The Lean
Enterprise
Memory Jogger™ for
Service

Where Supply Meets Demand... Exactly!

Richard L. MacInnes
Net Results, Inc.

First Edition | GOAL/QPC

The Lean Enterprise Memory Jogger™ for Service

Development Team
Susan Griebel, *Project Leader*
Rob King, *Illustrator*
Janet MacCausland, *Designer*
nSight, Inc., *Project Editor*

GOAL/QPC
12 Manor Parkway, Salem, NH 03079-2841
Toll free: **800.643.4316** or **603.893.1944**
Fax: 603.870.9122
E-mail: **service@goalqpc.com**
www.MemoryJogger.org

Printed in the United States of America

First Edition
10 9 8 7 6 5 4 3 2

ISBN: 978-1-57681-110-8

Acknowledgments

Our sincere thanks to the people and organizations who reviewed *The Lean Enterprise Memory Jogger™ for Service* and offered suggestions and encouragement. Their participation in the development process assured us that the tools and methods described in this book are relevant and appropriate for all associates to use in their quest to achieve a truly lean enterprise.

David Boyle,
Drummond Company

Adil Dalal, *Pinnacle Process*

Lisa DeNatale, *Starwood Hotels & Resorts Worldwide, Inc.*

Gene Gallant,
New England Confectionery (NECCO Candies)

John Gatt,
Department of Navy

Gregg Gordon,
Kronos Incorporated

Laurie Harbour
Harbour Felax Group

Elizabeth Keane
– Automotive Industry

Liz Keim, *Integrated Quality Resources, LLC*

Todd Pait
– Healthcare Industry

Steven Pollock
– Healthcare Industry

Chuck Thomas,
Southwest Airlines

Scott Walton,
Harbour Results Inc.

Linda Weiland, *Embry Riddle Aeronautic University*

Lean Enterprise Division of ASQ

David Behling, *CMQ/OE*

Wendy Gomez

Alan Mendelssohn, *CSSBB*

Frank Murdock

Tammy Miller, *PMP, CSSBB*

Chad Vincent, *CQE, CRE, CMQ/OE, CSSBB*

Forward

In today's highly competitive market, there is an intense drive to ensure that an organization's operations are as productive as possible. The benefits from becoming a "lean" organization include the freeing up of time and resources to focus on activities that matter most to the customer while improving the business bottom-line.

The tools and methods outlined in this book for optimizing resources, streamlining operations, and eliminating waste had their origins in manufacturing. Experience, however, has shown that these methods are applicable everywhere. For this reason, we have named this series of books *The Lean Enterprise Memory Jogger™ Series*.

We believe this book will enable associates at all levels to quickly learn and begin applying the most commonly used tools for creating value and eliminating waste.

We wish you well.

GOAL/QPC

Table of Contents

Special Note

As a highly specialized strategy and services firm, working with public- and private-sector industries around the globe, we truly understand the lean imperative as a business strategy. Taking time away from our pressing and often unpredictable business activities to prepare this memory jogger, has required tremendous sacrifice by all of my colleagues—Scott Walton, Lyda Camp, Valerie Bearden, and Don Smith. Their support throughout this project has been invaluable and deeply appreciated.

I would also like to thank all of the professionals at GOAL/QPC with whom I have enjoyed an incredible relationship. They are the real deal and know what it takes to help companies achieve the next level of success.

To all I say... "Thanks team!"

INTRODUCTION

What Is a Lean Enterprise?

As organizations and industries challenge themselves to improve in all aspects of their business and operational practices—from craft to mass to lean production, to the bigger concept of a lean enterprise—the evolution continues.

The term *lean production* was coined in 1988 by John Krafcik, a member of MIT's International Motor Vehicle Program (IMVP), which produced its research findings in the seminal work, "The Machine That Changed the World." This book explained that lean production, compared to mass production, required only "half the human effort in the factory, half the manufacturing space, half the investment in tools, half the engineering hours to develop a new product in half the time" (Womack, 13).

Lean enterprise was also coined by the IMVP to include all aspects of "product design and engineering, then going far beyond the factory to the customer" (Womack, 73). Lean enterprise principles and practices can be universally applied to the service industry; all services experience the same life cycle of design, delivery, and completion of all customer transactions. However, most service organizations need help converting specific lean philosophies and process methodologies to the service environment—the driving force behind this Memory Jogger™ pocket guide.

Why Lean?

Lean goals of defining demand, extending demand lead time, matching supply to demand, eliminating waste, reducing supply lead times, and reducing total costs when applied systematically will improve organizational performance in virtually all dimensions. This pocket guide will explore the details of a lean enterprise initiative. The bigger questions, however, have to be answered by leadership: Does your organization need to improve in order to compete more effectively in the marketplace? Have you achieved an absolute advantage in your marketplace?

Absolute Advantage is—a concept of trade in which an entity offers the exact products and services its customers demand and produces them efficiently, using fewer labor, and capital resources, than does its competition.

If there is room for improvement, then lean philosophies and methods will be extremely useful in focusing organizational resources on mutual success.

Benefits of Lean

Published research by the University of California, San Diego Extension has indicated that implementating lean principles have lead to dramatic improvements, such as:

◻ Production Cycle Time: 10 to 95 percent reduction

◻ Business Process Transaction Cycle Time: 50 to 90 percent reduction

- ◻ Inventory: 40 to 80 percent reduction

- ◻ Production Floor Space/Office Area: 30 to 60 percent reduction

- ◻ Productivity: 25 to 60 percent improvement

- ◻ New Product/Service Development Lead Time: 10 to 50 percent improvement

- ◻ Operating Costs: 15 to 25 percent reduction

- ◻ Cost of Poor Quality: 30 to 50 percent reduction

According to the research, "Many organizations waste 50 percent–70 percent of available resources through improper management of material, time, information, idle equipment, and inventory."

What Is a Lean Enterprise in the 21st Century?

The lean enterprise of the 21st century is on track to expertly match supply to demand, at the time of demand, at the place of demand, and at quality and quantity levels demanded—the first time, every time. With continued advances in communication and information technology, companies are able to perform information-centric services around the clock, anywhere in the world, much more efficiently than ever imagined. People, facilities, and/or special equipment-centric services are also being challenged to rethink the normal working hours, the usual practice of making customers wait for their turn in the queue, and the role of the customer in the service delivery process. It is an exciting time to be in business as customers, competitors, and organizations like yours strive for perfection in the marketplace.

Historically, organizations in all industries, in both the public sector and the private sector, have applied the principles and practices associated with the original tenets of lean enterprise forged by the Toyota Motor Company in the 1950s. That's right! More than forty years ago, Toyota sought a new solution to the challenges of resource constraints and the market requirement to produce a wide variety of automobiles in lesser volumes than the U.S. market produced. Toyota's storied progress and success have received much attention and study worldwide.

The 21st century lean system emphasizes the understanding of service demand, matching supply to demand, and the prevention of waste, or as Toyota would say, *muda*, meaning activity that is wasteful and does not add value. A lean system's unique tools, techniques, and methods can help your organization achieve just-in-time service delivery, extend demand lead time, and shorten supply lead times while simultaneously reducing costs. But to achieve these lean objectives a company must foster a culture in which all employees continually improve their skill levels and service processes.

What Is *Lean for Service*?

Simply put, Lean for Service is the application of lean philosophies, principles, and methodologies to the service environment.

What Is Service?

Service is generically defined as work done by one person or group that benefits another. According to the United States Census in 2008, the private non-good-producing industries account for approximately 70% of total economic activity. These non-good-producing industries include retail trade, wholesale trade, and the service industries.

Services activities, for the purpose of this pocket guide, are any services performed for a customer, external or internal. Each service has an output(s), requires inputs, and uses resources such as people, data, information technology, facilities, materials, equipment, and so on, acting under standardized work methods and instructions. To be clear, some service activities do produce a product, such as remanufacturing a product for resale or building or installing products in the customer environment. In summary, this pocket guide will focus on service delivery rather than traditional production applications.

Clarification: Service Offering Versus Service Process

A service performed for an external customer is an *offering*. The goals of the lean enterprise apply first and foremost to this offering. Internal business processes are often classified as services. For example—a service request to repair a computer failure, invoice reconciliation services, freight management services all have internal customers. In the lean organization it is important to distinguish between demand associated with external "service offerings" and the demands for internal "service processes." A well constructed enterprise map (Chapter 4) will ultimately link service offerings to service processes.

Clarification: Service Lean Versus Transactional Lean

Many companies have pursued lean services initiatives, others transactional lean. For the purposes of this pocket guide, we will apply lean concepts to both services and transactions. We will use the term service to represent both services and transactions.

The Lean Enterprise Transformation Roadmap

The Lean Enterprise Transformation Roadmap was crafted to provide general guidance in the use of the tools contained in this pocket guide. It also references essential lean elements commonly associated with manufacturing practices, which are addressed in greater detail in *The Lean Enterprise Memory Jogger™ for Production*.

The Lean Enterprise Transformation Roadmap is designed to support a complete organization transformation beginning with Lean Goals organized into a process, Lean Leadership that directs organizational change, and the use of the Enterprise Mapping method to identify opportunities

Lean Enterprise Transformation Roadmap

Value Stream Optimization

Lean Goals Ch1	Lean Leadership Ch2	Enterprise Mapping Ch3	Standard Operations Ch9	Lean Metrics Ch10	Kaizen Events Ch11
		Value Stream Mapping Ch4	Continuous Flow Ch5	Queuing Strategies Ch6	Kanban LEMJ – Production

Lean Foundational Capabilities

Visual Management Ch7	Error Proofing Ch8	Quick Changeover LEMJ – Production	Total Productive Maintenance LEMJ – Production

for lean improvements. Ultimately, new practices comprise Standard Operations that guide lean operations while Lean Metrics monitor performance and drive ongoing Kaizen Events to improve localized practices.

The Lean Enterprise Transformation Roadmap suggests the use of Value Stream Mapping, Continuous Flow, and Queuing Strategies to optimize the specific value streams that comprise the enterprise. Kanban, a defined method for controlling the sequencing, quantity, and control of work, is touched upon here but explained more fully in *The Lean Enterprise Memory Jogger™ for Production*.

The Lean Enterprise Transformation Roadmap identifies foundational capabilities that must be present in an organization to achieve lean: building intelligence into the work environment through Visual Management and preventing errors that cause defects through Error Proofing methods. Also referenced are Quick Changeover to ensure smaller lot sizes with reduced downtime and Total Productive Maintenance methods to ensure availability of critical equipment. Both of these are also explained in detail in *The Lean Enterprise Memory Jogger™ for Production*.

How to Use This Book

This book will explain what you need to know to transform your organization into a lean enterprise. The specific information it provides includes:

□ Concepts and definitions you need to know

□ Skills you need to develop

□ Tools you need to use

□ Steps you need to take

Armed with these tools you and your team will be able to work together systematically toward your lean-enterprise goals.

What Do the Icons Mean?

 Topics of special interest to lean team leaders are marked with this icon. Your workforce may choose to skip these sections.

Topics that are best addressed by an entire team working together are marked with this icon.

To Find the Start of Each Chapter

Look for the solid box at the bottom of the page near the page number.

To Find Special Tips

Look for the areas with the TIP icon shown.

Chapter ONE

THE GOALS OF THE LEAN ENTERPRISE

Lean Goals – the goals are sequenced to reflect a connected process for achieving lean.

1. Define demand for services
2. Extend demand lead time
3. Match supply to demand
4. Eliminate waste
5. Reduce supply lead time
6. Reduce total costs

The universal key performance indicators (KPIs) of quality, cost, and delivery are not lost on the lean enterprise; in fact they are front and center. A lean enterprise meets these KPIs through a series of cascading goals that focus organizational efforts.

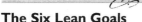

The Six Lean Goals

What if the following lean goals were organized as a sequence, meaning you understood demand before you defined supply and, ultimately, eliminated waste? In the bigger scheme, Goal 1: Define Demand for Service is just as important as Goal 6: Reduce Total Costs. However, without a clear understanding of demand it is hard to successfully align resources and optimize processes.

Goal 1: Define Demand for Services

Quite simply, this means defining the desire of purchasers, consumers, internal customers, and so on, for services. Services must be consistently delivered per customer expectations in order to ensure business success. When defining demand it is important to understand the multiple dimensions of customer expectations. Does the service meet the specific "content" requirements (the ability to repair a computer)? Can the service be delivered when and where the customer desires (in my office; within the next sixty minutes)? Does the customer's experience with the service provider meet expectations (courteous, active listener, thorough, professional appearance)?

Ultimately, the nature of demand—what is demanded, how much, how frequently, by whom, where, when, and so on—guides decisions on how demand will be met and what the supply chain must look like to deliver to demand. Without a deep understanding of these dimensions an organization will find it quite difficult to creating a lean enterprise.

Goal 2: Extend Demand Lead Time

In the service environment, statistics are used to characterize and forecast demand. The best statistic is one that reflects a known demand and ample time to respond to it. Organizations must build into their efforts the sensing and forecasting mechanisms that give them the earliest possible demand information. By extending demand lead time, companies give themselves flexibility to combine and schedule their resources to match supply to demand.

Goal 3: Match Supply to Demand

The third goal of a lean enterprise is to match the supply of its service offerings to the demands of an ever-changing marketplace. It is essential that a company continuously assess its ability to meet existing and emerging customer expectations (as described in Goal 1) and use demand input to design how it will make resources available in response to demand. In the perfect lean organization, demand and supply are matched exactly.

In the service environment, organizations constrain supply by how they set their operational hours and make the necessary resources available. Without access to an affordable and infinite supply of resources, at any time and any place, customers have either learned to wait, learned to do it themselves, or simply lived without the desired service. Bottom line: A lean enterprise must focus on matching supply to demand to increase customer satisfaction and to gain competitive advantage in the marketplace.

Goal 4: Eliminate Waste

Waste is defined as any activity that doesn't create value for the organization or its customers. Much ado has been made about internal services that are essential business capabilities being classified by traditional "lean" definitions as non-value-adding and, thus, a waste. For example, it makes business sense that a company needs processes to recruit, hire and develop its people. How could these processes be classified as non-value-adding? The industry has responded by developing multiple "good business sense" definitions of value. Let's quickly review them.

Value-Adding (Value Creating)

In traditional lean applications, a *value-adding* activity directly affects service offerings. This definition has been expanded to encompass all the value-creating activities of a business such as all transactions that support order fulfillment activities and business activities that deliver vital resource capabilities which in turn enable the service delivery.

The broader concept of *value creating* has been adopted as organizations begin to understand that people, data, information technology, facilities, tools, equipment, and work methods are often deployed in combination to deliver services. For example, the human resource management function delivers qualified and capable resources to deliver services, and maintenance resources ensure that equipment is reliable and available to perform.

Non-Value-Adding (Value Destroying)

A *non-value-adding* activity does not add value to the offerings or an essential business capability. Waste such as waiting, extra processing, and defects are examples of *non-value-adding* activities.

The broader concept of *value destroying* is any activity or supporting resource that is wasteful and/or not useful to the performance of the necessary core, enabling, and ad hoc processes of the organization. The phrase value destroying is used in conjunction with value creating to classify an activity.

Goal 5: Reduce Supply Lead Time

Supply lead time is the total time it takes to complete a series of tasks within a process or combination of processes in order to deliver a service in response to a customer demand. Lead time consists of task cycle times and periods of waiting, which are classified as batch delays and process delays. Examples of lead time include the period between the receipt of a sales order and when the customer's payment is received, the time it takes to request maintenance support to the completion of the work order, and, on an enterprise level, the time it takes to introduce new services after they are first designed.

By reducing supply lead time, a lean enterprise improves its ability to match supply to demand, respond to changes in customer demand, increase capacity to handle multiple demands more efficiently, improve planning and scheduling flexibility, and improve response time to unplanned events.

For some organizations this goal drives their entire lean initiative as it is believed that supply lead time reduction, by design, drives resource efficiency.

Goal 6: Reduce Total Costs

In economic terms a lean enterprise is one that strives for an absolute advantage in the marketplace. The absolute advantage is a concept of trade in which an entity delivers services more efficiently, using fewer labor and/or capital resources than its competition.

Any investments in excess resources, such as people, materials, and equipment, or in inefficient processes are considered wastes. Conversely, not applying enough of the right types and amount of resources to meet service demands would also be a waste. By investing in lean principles and methods, an organization eliminates the costs of wasteful activities.

Bringing It All Together

A lean enterprise is a customer-driven organization that derives its value from the services it offers to the market, the resources it provides to its associates, and the culture of its work environment. It is not coincidence that the six goals exist: Define what the customer wants (demand), ascertain demand requirements at the earliest possible time, match supply to demand requirements, drive out wastes that consume valuable resources, increase organization flexibility by reducing lead time, and focus investments in organizational capabilities that create versus destroy value.

Making It Happen

It is impossible to develop the perfect practical path forward for each of these lean goals. What follows are high-level guidelines to use as thought starters.

Achieving Goal 1: Define Demand for Services

Perhaps the most challenging test of a lean enterprise is developing a true understanding of how much and how often customers will desire services. The typical lean initiative begins with understanding the nature of customer demands. The nature of demand goes beyond the nature of the service "event" itself; it also includes all of the supporting business transactions. For example, if a customer requires his car to be serviced, associated business transactions may include scheduling the service, ordering parts if required, billing the customer, processing a credit card transaction, and so on. Understanding the nature of demand will help guide the lean initiative as you design and optimize supply.

How do I do it?

1. Begin your lean initiative activities. Understand your customers' demands by conducting a

Process-Quantity (P_cQ) analysis. The P_cQ analysis (Chapter 5) should be conducted to quantify the nature of both customers and their demands. P typically stands for Product; however, in a service or transaction world P_c stands for Process. Q stands for Quantity.

2. Make logical decisions on how you segment your P_cQ analysis. Every service offering and internal service process has an output. These outputs may be variations or subsets of other outputs (e.g., *repair computer*, *repair computer keyboard*, and *replace computer battery*). Look for logical groupings of processes and transactions at the highest levels first before flowing down to next levels of detail.

3. Make sure you have operationally defined the processes and transactions and fully understand who the customers are and what demands are being met by the offering or service. For example, *repair computer* may not be sufficient. *Repair [brand name] laptop computer* may be more useful for understanding demand.

4. Analyze demand patterns of the service offering, such as the potential demand (maximum/minimum) for any service per day/week/month; actual demand; future demand; and evolutionary demand driven by changes in service offerings. Review demand frequency often to determine consistent timing patterns upon which to deliver offerings or internal services. Determine the demand for each offering and each major process of an internal service.

5. Conduct a statistical analysis to determine if demand can be modeled or simulated. Use results to forecast future demand.

6. Estimate takt time for demand (see Chapter 10 for information on how to calculate demand).

Achieving Goal 2: Extend Demand Lead Time

Demand lead time is the period between when a customer's demand is known and when it is communicated to the source of supply. The sooner the supply source knows that an actual demand exists, the sooner it can begin its resource planning and scheduling activities. By extending demand lead time and reducing supply lead time, the customer gains access to the right service at the right time and the supplier gains the most flexibility in responding to demand.

How do I do it?

1. Understand the nature of demand per Goal 1.

2. Determine the demand drivers for service offerings by capturing market and sales data on what created the demand.

3. Determine the demand drivers for service processes by capturing activity data on what created the demand.

4. Determine the causes that create the demand.

Can these causes be analyzed to determine likely patterns? These causes become demand drivers that can guide business and operational decisions.

5. Determine if the causes of the demand can be predicted or planned.

6. Establish business or operational practices that enable the organization to sense changes in demand. This may include collaborative planning and forecasting (CPFR) efforts with customers. Provide communication channels so that customers can express needs before service times.

 If demand is created by a piece of equipment or information technology, consider the use of condition-based monitoring techniques for advanced warning of demand.

7. Integrate demand information into service planning and scheduling activities.

Achieving Goal 3: Match Supply to Demand

The lean system tries to make supply resources available at the right time and in the right capacity to match demand requirements. The frequency of demand is "owned" by the customer. When and how much supply will be made available is "owned" by the service provider. Takt time is derived from these two factors. Ultimately, service delivery is sequenced and resources are balanced to meet takt time estimates.

How do I do it?

1. Construct a process route based on the results of the P_cQ analysis table to determine if services can be grouped by like activities.

2. Apply queuing strategies to determine the best approach to sequencing and executing services to match supply to demand.

3. Apply continuous flow methods to design the optimal sequence of service activities, estimate resource requirements, and forecast supply lead time to minimize customer wait time.

4. Create and develop a standard operations combination chart for offerings in order to understand the components of work, associated cycle times, and sources of lead time wastes.

5. Prepare a standard work flow diagram based on input from the process route diagram in order to determine if activities can be physically organized to improve flow.

6. Conduct a capacity analysis based on known demand drivers for service resources (human, materials, technology, equipment, etc.). Distribute resource-based lean service requirements and design.

7. Develop standard operations to guide the performance of offerings and internal services.

8. Evaluate performance using the applicable metrics of effectiveness, efficiency, cycle time, and total investment.

Achieving Goal 4: Eliminate Waste

To eliminate waste, begin by imagining a perfect service offering or process in which the following conditions exist:

◻ Services are produced only to fill a customer demand.

◻ There is immediate response to customer needs.

◻ There are zero service defects.

◻ Delivery to the customer is instantaneous.

◻ The service is delivered with the optimal combination of resources, such as people, processes, and technology, to achieve the lowest possible cost.

By imagining a perfect operation like this, you will begin to see how much waste is hidden in your company. Using lean initiatives will enable you to eliminate that waste and get closer to a perfect operation.

The Eight Types of Waste

As you use the tools and techniques of the lean enterprise, you will work to eliminate eight types of waste, which are defined below:

◻ *Overservicing*. The worst type of waste, overservicing, occurs when we deliver offerings or perform services that are simply not needed. In the lean environment, it is important to perform services per customer timing expectations and per scheduled use of resources, but no sooner and no later. The results of overservicing are 1) clients being overcharged for the benefit they receive, 2) internal resources being tied up with less productive activities, and 3) increased internal costs with no benefit.

◻ *Waiting*. Also known as *queuing*, this term refers to periods of inactivity by the customer or a service process. Idle customers who lack control over their waiting time may quickly become dissatisfied. Internal service resources who find themselves waiting are often used in alternate activities that don't add value, are not high priority, or don't leverage their skills.

◻ *Transport*. This is the unnecessary movement of resources, such as people, tools, equipment, materials, and documents, from one service activity to another or one service location to another. Transportation can consume a tremendous amount of time and resources, during which potentially no value-added activity is being performed.

□ **Extra Processing.** This term refers to extra operations, such as unnecessary levels of decision making, rework, reprocessing, handling, and storage, that occur because of defects, overservicing, or too many or too few available resources to perform those services. It is more efficient to complete a process correctly the first time rather than make time to do it over to correct errors.

□ **Inventory.** This refers to any excess inventory that is not directly required for delivery of offerings and performance of internal services. In the service environment, physical inventory consists of all supply resources such as excess materials, equipment, and facilities. Inventory can be virtual as well, for instance, a backlog of work or tasks to be accomplished.

□ **Motion.** This refers to the extra steps taken by employees and equipment to accommodate inefficient process layouts, defects (see next bullet point), reprocessing, overservicing, and too little or too much inventory. Like transport, motion takes time and adds no value to your service.

□ **Defects.** These are aspects of your service that do not conform to your customers' expectations or internal requirements, thus causing customer dissatisfaction. Defects have hidden costs, such as those incurred by multiple service deliveries, dispute resolution, lost sales, and poor employee morale. Defects can occur in the service offering and in the resources used, for instance, materials, methods, technology, tools, and so on. They can also include interactions with the service provider and business transactions such as ordering, scheduling, payment, and any follow-up support.

◻ *Lack of Employee Involvement and Creativity.* In today's ever-changing environment, organizations have realized that perhaps the most hidden waste is not tapping into the known—and often unknown—capabilities of its associates. It refers to the human capability to expertly perform tasks, to analyze and improve work processes, and to acquire skills required to deliver new service offerings and adapt to emerging operational practices.

How do I do it?

1. Before you launch a series of waste-reduction initiatives, consider constructing an enterprise map (Chapter 3) that reflects service offerings as well as service processes and their current performance against demand requirements. Use of a big picture approach helps identify lean initiative candidates in which improving services provides the best return for the invested effort.

2. Coordinate team-based waste-reduction activities based on the identification of services that are ineffective, that are inefficient, and that require excess investments to perform.

3. Identify associated processes that perform poorly or need performance improvement. If

appropriate, focus on the operation in your organization with the highest customer dissatisfaction or lowest internal performance ratings.

4. Using the enterprise map as the baseline, create a value stream map that further details the operation you are reviewing (Chapter 4).

5. Review the value stream map to identify the location, magnitude, and frequency of the eight types of waste associated with the offering or service activity.

6. Establish metrics for identifying the magnitude and frequency of waste associated with this operation (Chapter 10).

7. Begin your problem-solving efforts by using lean principles to reduce or eliminate the waste.

8. Periodically review the effectiveness, efficiency, cycle time, and investment metrics you have identified to continue eliminating waste associated with this operation.

9. Repeat this process with other lean initiative candidates' offerings or internal service activities in your organization.

Achieving Goal 5: Reduce Supply Lead Time

Reducing lead time, the time from start to finish that it takes to complete an activity, is one of the most effective ways to reduce waste and lower total costs. Lead time can be broken down into three basic components:

1. *Cycle time.* This is the time it takes to complete the tasks required for a single work process, such as performing equipment maintenance or completing a sales order.

2. *Batch delay.* This is the time during which a service activity is idle while other services or transactions are completed or processed. An example is the time the first service request of the day is on hold while all the other service requests for that day are entered into the system to await approval.

3. *Process delay.* This is the lag time during which batches must wait after one operation ends and the next one begins. Continuing the batch delay example, a process delay occurs when a service request backlog in the computer is awaiting approval by local supervisors and then by service management supervisors, and for high-cost service orders, for upper level management approval. It could take days, if not weeks, to get a service order through process delays.

> **Tip** The distinction between demand lead time and supply lead time is critical. The goal is to extend demand lead time while reducing supply lead time. This gives your organization the most flexibility in matching supply to demand. Both lead times have cycle time, batch, and process delay components.

How do I do it?

The steps your improvement team must take to reduce lead time are similar to the ones you take to eliminate waste.

1. Before you launch a series of lead-time reduction initiatives, consider constructing an enterprise map (Chapter 3) that reflects service offerings as well as service processes and their current performance against demand requirements. Using a big picture approach, focus on identifying lean initiative candidates where improving lead times of offerings or internal services provide the best return for the invested effort.

2. Team-based lead-time reduction activities should be used to create a value stream map, as an extension of your enterprise mapping efforts, for the service process you are targeting (Chapter 4).

3. Calculate the time required for the value-added steps of the process. This represents the best-case time for the service process as it is currently designed.

4. Review the value stream map to identify where you can reduce lead time. Brainstorm ways to make the total lead time equal the time required for the value-added steps that you calculated in step 2.

5. Apply queuing strategies to improve lead time.

6. Determine what constraints exist in the process and develop a plan to either eliminate them or manage them more efficiently.

7. Apply continuous flow strategies to improve lead time.

8. Establish metrics to identify the location, duration, and frequency of lead times within the process (Chapter 10).

9. Once you have established a plan for improving the process, measure the improvement.

10. Repeat this process for other inefficient operations in your organization.

Achieving Goal 6: Reduce Total Costs

As stated previously, businesses must invest in capabilities and each investment has an associated cost. But what service offerings or service processes should a company invest in and what is the right amount of investment? The lean enterprise makes these investment decisions a function of customer demand requirements and the optimal supply design and resource configuration. Total costs are the sum investments that the resources need to deliver service offerings and perform service processes.

This is an exciting time in the industry as breakthrough methods have made their way into the marketplace, enabling firms to value both their tangible and intangible assets. With this knowledge, companies can now guide their investment decisions not only by how much the offerings will cost to deliver, but by what the cost to the firms will be if they deliver it poorly, thus affecting their reputation and brand in the marketplace. Furthermore, companies establish a poor work environment if they don't promote employee excellence; the subsequent financial impact will be on employee retention and recruitment.

Cost-Optimization Methods

Use one or more of the methods listed to identify places to optimize the costs related to your company's current processes or services. These methods are useful for analyzing and allocating costs during the new service-design process.

◻ **Target Pricing.** Target pricing focuses on how the customer perceives the worth of the service being offered. They often determine worth by looking at comparable services or alternatives available in the market. It's important to remember that pricing has an effect on your sales volumes and, thus, on your service volumes. The rise and fall of service volumes affect investment strategies and cost management activities—ultimately determining the profitability of your company.

◻ **Target Costing.** This involves determining the investment costs at which a future service must be produced so that it can generate the desired profits. Target costing is broken down into three main components: service, resources required, and internal and external operations. This, in turn, helps designers to break down cost factors.

◻ **Value Engineering.** This is a systematic examination of service cost factors, taking into account the target quality standards and the price. Value engineering studies assign cost factors by taking into account what the service does to meet customer expectations. These studies also estimate the relative value of each "dimension" of the service over its life cycle. The following techniques are useful for analyzing and improving the cost of your organization's service operations.

- ¤ *Activity-Based Costing (ABC).* ABC systems allocate investments costs—first to activities and processes and then to services and customers. For example, a company may employ this technique to determine how much investment in purchasing capabilities should be allocated to offerings (buying tools to complete customer services) or to internal business process (buying tools to conduct internal maintenance activities).

- ¤ *Kaizen (i.e., continuous improvement) Costing.* Kaizen focuses on driving lead time and waste-reduction activities, which, by design, reduce the investment costs of delivering offerings to the market or of performing internal services.

- ¤ *Cost Maintenance.* This monitors how well your company's operations adhere to the cost standards set by the engineering, operations, finance, or accounting departments after they conduct target costing and Kaizen-costing activities.

How do I do it?

1. Cost optimization activities should be built onto all lean initiatives.

2. Before you launch a series of cost optimization initiatives, consider constructing an enterprise map (Chapter 3) that reflects service offerings, as well as service processes and their current performance, against demand requirements. Using a big picture approach, focus on identifying lean initiative candidates that offer the best return for the invested effort by improving the investment costs of offerings or internal services.

3. Decide whether your cost optimization efforts will begin with a new or existing offering. Also do this for a new or existing internal service.

4. Use target pricing, target costing, or value engineering if new service offerings are the focus of your improvement efforts..

5. Apply ABC costing, Kaizen costing, or cost maintenance if existing service offerings are your focus. Begin by reviewing your company's high-investment cost capabilities.

Tip
If your service offering or internal service process is inherently costly, first consider applying the lean enterprise techniques identified in this book, then focus your efforts on reducing total costs. Typically, this will involve companywide participation.

LEAN LEADERSHIP

What Is Lean Leadership?

Successful lean organizations deliver superior service while creating meaningful work. Furthermore, they meet bottom-line objectives by managing on-going investment in the right resources. Resources like people, processes, information technology, data, facilities, equipment, and tools—both internal and external—dedicated to the mission of the organization. What distinguishes lean leadership from other forms of leadership is its ability to combine and sequence resources, in the most effective and efficient manner, and to match supply to demand—exactly!

Preparing for the Future While Optimizing the Present

The lean goal of matching supply to demand challenges leadership to continuously sense changes in customer and market demands and, subsequently, to reconfigure and realign resources to achieve the same. It also drives continuous evaluation of new business philosophies, technology, methods, and so on, which provide capabilities previously not available. For example, who would have imagined the far-reaching effect of internet technology on today's service environment? Who would have thought the Toyota Production System, an intangible asset, would revolutionize both cultural and operational models across the globe?

Having a constant eye on the future, however, does not relieve management of the responsibility to stay focused on the tasks at hand. For most organizations, demand for services fluctuates daily, resources come and go, new competitive challenges arise, and government and industry regulations change. And just when the processes and resources are dialed in, someone or something moves the needle. Thus the lean standardized processes have an evolving life as well.

Addressing the Challenges of Change

Numerous models have been deployed to effectively cascade business strategies into operational practices, to select and guide both project and individual improvement activities, and to effectively manage the dynamics of change that these initiatives invariably create. This pocket guide will briefly introduce common tenets of change management and suggest some practical considerations for deploying a lean initiative.

Change Management Principles

Change Management Principles
1. Leadership must lead
2. Know where you are headed
3. First things first
4. Change must be compelling
5. Don't go it alone
6. Commit to successful action
7. Achieve measured success
8. Never stop

Leadership Must Lead

There is a fine line between delegation and abdication. Lean leadership does not abdicate the responsibility to improve the organization by handing it over to a single person or department. It engages the entirety of the organization in the improvement process. It selects and directs organizational improvement initiatives through conscientious evaluation of service offerings and internal capabilities. It then sponsors and, where appropriate, delegates the leadership of change initiative to the associates of the organization. The lean goals and the enterprise mapping process described herein are designed to help leadership direct the lean transformation process from a strategic perspective.

Know Where You Are Headed

Leadership must be able to answer the question: Is the change undertaken indeed moving the organization in the right direction? Remarkably, answering this question is not as easy you might think. In his book *Future Perfect*, Stan Davis introduces the concepts of Any Time, Any Place, No-Matter, and Mass Customization as general directions for products and services. Simply put, in the future services must be delivered at the time demand for them occurs and at the place that demand occurs, and they must instantly take the form required by the customer, in essence matching supply to demand—exactly. Impractical? Maybe. Directionally correct? *Absolutely*. These standards of perfection are used to compare whether the lean process improvements are moving you in the right direction.

First Things First

Leadership understands that it has finite resources to carry out its three fundamental business activities: do business, improve how one does business, and prepare the business for the future. In the lean enterprise there is a particular focus on understanding *demand* first and *supply* second. If demand is changing, leadership must question, and then analyze, how this affects its organization. Perhaps the harder question to answer is, *How can an organization match supply to demand if it does not know the demand?* Once demand is known, the lean challenge is to configure supply resources to best meet demand at the lowest invested cost.

Chapter 1, "Lean Goals," defined the sequential path forward: *doing first things first*. Practically speaking, the enterprise map (Chapter 3) and supporting value stream maps (Chapter 4) begin the alignment of supply to demand. Each subsequent lean tool helps you *do right things right* to achieve optimization, organization, and standardization of supply practices. Selecting which lean initiative to undertake and in what order is not a function of a weighted voting exercise; it is based on a systematic analysis of offerings (demand) and current practices (supply) that will provide the best return on investment for any given lean initiative.

Change Must Be Compelling

We often lament that it takes a crisis to make change a reality. Why waste a good crisis? It is commonly understood that the pain for staying the same must exceed the pain for change. So if not enough pain exists, create it. Inject conflict, raise the bar, and create big, audacious goals. This approach creates harmony and focus! What… are you kidding??? Lean initiatives in this environment cannot be sustained.

Lean organizations integrate the need for change into the very fiber of their thinking and doing. They are no less demanding on achieving results than a crisis-led organization, but they are more demanding on the knowledge of the process and what needs to be changed to achieve it. As demand changes, so must supply—this is obvious! As resource capabilities (people, technology, tools, equipment) change there is constant reevaluation of how they can be reconfigured to improve performance and reduce total cost. This is also obvious! Lean companies make change compelling through their rewards and recognition processes, whereby changing the organization is seen as a requirement and crisis management is seen as the last option. The resulting culture of improvement is not driven by fear but by success.

Don't Go It Alone

Leadership must lead, but the associates of the organization must be skillfully trained and engaged if the lean initiative is to be successful. Skill development is driven by the knowledge that the strength of a lean system is dependent on its weakest link. Who is engaged depends on what is to be improved. Lean initiatives can occur on many system levels, such as extended enterprise, enterprise, system, process, function, and task levels. Lean initiatives also require people to play different roles:

□ *Those who work in the system.* They understand the content of current work and all of its associated challenges. They are masters of their work.

□ *Those who work on the system.* They understand the theory and logic of best practices and to what extent best practices can be applied to the organization. They are masters of best practices and benchmarks, regardless of industry.

□ *Those who know the lean and six sigma tools.* They understand the specific application of lean (process optimization) and six sigma (variation reduction) tools contained herein and in other writings. They are masters of process improvement methodologies.

□ *Those who know how to facilitate change through people.* They understand the tenets of change management and work tirelessly to integrate these into the lean enterprise and its initiatives. They understand people, what motivates them, and how to align personal objectives with that of the organization. They are the masters of organizational psychology and change management methodologies.

□ *Those who know how to manage project teams.* They understand the orderly progression and interdependency of tasks based on priorities and availability of necessary resources. They balance the need to make vital change happen as quickly as possible without diminishing the organization's ability to deliver its services to the marketplace. They are masters of project tasks, resources, and time management.

Although each and every role cited above is necessary to your initiative, that doesn't mean that numerous individuals are necessary to fulfill each of the roles. Just be sure that these capabilities exist in your organization or you will indeed be going it alone.

Commit to Successful Action

Gaining commitment is perhaps the toughest challenge to leading a successful lean transformation. As suggested earlier, we can create or leverage crises and/or we can drive commitment by using integrated lean goals that enable us to systematically match supply to demand.

It is much easier to commit to a lean initiate if one has explicit knowledge that the change being pursued is indeed an improvement and if the methods for improving skills, leveraging technology, rearranging workflows, and so on can be explained, mapped, and demonstrated. It simply makes sense.

Lacking explicit knowledge, one must have trust that leadership is correct in asking stakeholders to engage in a lean initiative. Here achieving commitment is much more challenging. The associates engaged in the lean initiatives must know—through communication, education, understanding, and direct engagement in a lean project—why they are being asked to commit to a certain course of action, that is why it benefits them and the organization. In all cases, the responsibility for lean enterprise success rests with leadership. Leadership must lead, understand the merits of the change, understand that leadership can't go it alone, communicate direction, and manage change.

Achieve Measured Success

Leadership must adopt two general classifications of metrics to ensure successful lean enterprise transformation. The first is metrics of the Present: present performance effectiveness, resource efficiencies, process lead-times, and total costs. The second is metrics of the Future: future-oriented metrics used to evaluate the organization in ways that enable it to meet emerging requirements of the marketplace and investor expectations. Combining the enterprise map (Chapter 3) with the structured metrics approach defined in Chapter 10 "Lean Metrics" provides the necessary framework for both present- and future-oriented metrics.

Never Stop

It is not enough to measure present performance and identify gaps in future capabilities; there is an implicit goal to use metrics to drive systematic and sustainable improvements. Lean analytics combine metrics with a structured approach to organize and lead ongoing improvement initiatives. Lean leadership's goal is not to go from crisis to crisis, but to invest in resources that drive sustainable improvements, thus guaranteeing success now and into the future. This requires an overall lean initiative structure that works on as well as in the system. The structure and content of this *Lean Enterprise Memory Jogger™ for Service* is designed to assist your organization in achieving this structure.

The Lean Enterprise Memory Jogger™ for Service | ©2009 GOAL/QPC

Chapter THREE

ENTERPRISE MAPPING

An enterprise map is a high-level diagram of the internal services activities of an organization. An extended enterprise map depicts service offerings (service performed for an external customer) as well as the services of suppliers (their offerings to a buying organization). The enterprise map depicts both service tasks and associated transactions using simple block diagrams, activity icons (if desired), and arrows. Each element of the enterprise map may be color coded to represent the current effectiveness, efficiency, and level of integration, rendering a one-page snapshot of both the strengths and weaknesses of an enterprise as it designs, plans for, and delivers services.

Why use it?

- Readily identifies the scope of the service process and associated functions that, if improved, can provide the biggest benefit for effort expended.

- Helps teams understand the extent to which services interact with various parts of the organization and the supply chain.

- Helps teams more accurately define the value of the service and its associated information, in many forms.

- Enables the team to organize all the major resources—people, information technology, equipment, policies, procedures, and so on—according to their use in the natural flow of service activities.

- Highlights gaps, duplications, and misunderstandings between different functional areas.

- Improves team decision making by building a shared understanding and acceptance of current practices, while imagining a desired future state.

- Provides the basis for more detailed value stream mapping activities (Chapter 4).

What does it do?

The enterprise map helps teams understand what and how service activities are performed and integrated as a whole process. The enterprise map is an exceptional team-based method to readily identify current strengths and weaknesses while imagining an improved future state. The enterprise map can be used to depict both internal services and service offerings.

 Because the enterprise map provides the big picture view of several interconnected activities that comprise a service and its associated transactions, it is tempting to dive into the details—too deep and too fast. Details of specific service processes and functions should be further described using value stream mapping (Chapter 4) and flowcharting techniques (refer to *The Problem Solving Memory Jogger*™) while referencing their placement in the bigger enterprise map.

Example: SERV-ALL is a regional company that offers brand-name equipment repair services to both commercial and consumer accounts. Repair services are performed by its multiple service shops (equipment comes to the  shop) and by field services (technician goes to the equipment). SERV-ALL has recently begun its lean enterprise initiative. Its initiate is driven by

the service response requirements of equipment
manufacturers, advances in equipment technology
(outpacing current in-house capabilities), high-cost
operations, and a highly competitive marketplace.
SERV-ALL takes its first step by creating an enterprise map.

How do I do it?

1. Select a natural group of internal services or
   service offerings to map. This can be done as
   an extension of normal strategic, business, or
   improvement planning activities.

 A natural grouping of services can be arrived
at through the use of an affinity diagram. (Refer
to *The Memory Jogger™ II*).

 Consider reviewing an entire department's
or operations' services at the enterprise level,
versus a single service or offering.

 The P_cQ analysis and subsequent process
route diagram will aid in ordering a variety of
services. Ultimately you may optimize a specific
service using a value stream map (Chapter 4).

2. Assemble a team that understands the demand drivers, inputs, functional requirements,
   and content of the selected service activities.

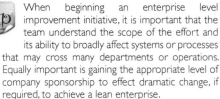

When beginning an enterprise level improvement initiative, it is important that the team understand the scope of the effort and its ability to broadly affect systems or processes that may cross many departments or operations. Equally important is gaining the appropriate level of company sponsorship to effect dramatic change, if required, to achieve a lean enterprise.

3. Assemble markers and Post-it™ Notes for a high-level mapping exercise. Alternatively, a very large whiteboard may work for this exercise.

4. Draw the large blocks of activities that occur in the service delivery process. Be mindful of core, enabling, and ad hoc processes that exist to ensure the proper delivery of the service.

   ▫ *Core processes*—activities, functions, and tasks, and so on that are inherent to the delivery of the service.

   ▫ *Enabling processes*—activities, functions, tasks, and so on that support the delivery of the service.

   ▫ *Ad hoc processes*—undocumented, uncontrolled, or not readily apparent activities, functions, tasks, and so on that can significantly affect the performance and cost of core and enabling process.

5. Begin mapping the enterprise by working backward from customer offerings or department/operational outputs through the major service activities.

Although team discussion may be detailed, the enterprise map should not be. Stay at the highest level descriptions; do not be tempted to go too deep too fast.

For extended enterprise maps, consider framing the mapping exercise using a Six Sigma SIPOC (Supplier Input Process Output Customer) diagram. Refer to *The Six Sigma Memory Jogger™ II* for guidance on the SIPOC diagram.

 Take your time to gather proof of how things are done. This may require that team members interview specific service providers, review documents, observe practices, and so on.

6.   Add activity flow arrows to your enterprise map.

 Example: SERV-ALL begins its enterprise mapping activity by identifying the highest level description of its equipment repair service functions for both core and enabling processes. It creates the draft of an enterprise map on page 39.

7.   Assess the current capability of each service function identified in your enterprise map. Capability is defined as the "ability to do something." Here are some common dimensions of capability that are assessed during the enterprise mapping activity. Refer to Chapter 10, "Lean Metrics," for additional measures and examples.

   □ Effectiveness—producing a desired or intended result.

   □ Efficiency—working productively with minimum wasted effort or expense.

   □ Cycle Time—the time it takes to perform functions correctly and in the correct sequence.

Serv-All Core Processes

Sales	Service Request	Service – Delivery Shops	Service – Delivery Field	Payment Transactions
Commercial Accounts	Electronic Based Requests	Service Lanes	Serv-All Inspections	Electronic Transactions
Consumers	Telephone Based Requests	Repair Bays	Contract Field Repairs	Manual Transactions

Serv-All Enabling Processes

Business Planning	Human Resources	Information Services	Contract Management	Facility Management
Marketing Plan	Staffing Plan	Business Operating System	Field Service Providers	Facility Design
Financial Plan	Employee Development	Diagnostic Systems		Facility Management
Resource Plan		Telecommunication System		

Materials Management	Quality Assurance	Work Methods	Fleet Management	Accounting
Inventory Management	Material Quality	Work Standards	Equipment Rentals	Budget
Warehouse Management	Service Quality	Policies and Procedures	Vehicle Acquisition and Maintenance	Accounts Payable
				Accounts Receivable

- **Integration**—the ability of the output (O) of one service activity to flow uninterrupted as an input (I) to another service activity. Similarly, integration is the ability of information to flow uninterrupted between applications or resources.

- **Total Costs**—the amount invested in resources required to deliver the service offering or perform the service process.

Capability assessment ratings attempt to stratify performance against the dimensions cited above. Here are two examples:

- **Numerical Rating Scheme** (based on fact-based sigma levels; the higher score the better):

  - 5—Meets expectations at six sigma level (3.4 defects per million)

  - 4—Meets expectations at five sigma level (233 defects per million)

  - 3—Meets expectations at four sigma level (6210 defects per million)

  - 2—Meets expectation at three sigma level (66,807 defects per million)

  - 1—Meets expectations at two sigma level (308,537 defects per million)

- **Color Rating Scheme** (based on a combination of fact-based and anecdotal evidence):

  - *Green*—performance trends in effectiveness, efficiency, cycle time, and total costs are improving and are considered a strength.

□ Yellow—performance trends in effectiveness, efficiency, cycle time, and total costs are stable but are considered a target for performance improvement.

□ Red—performance trends in effectiveness, efficiency, cycle time, and total costs are poor or worsening and require immediate attention.

Tip Rating protocols should be established for multiple trends and color ratings interpretations. For example, you may find effectiveness and efficiency trends going up (positive direction) and cost trends going up (negative direction). Your team may also rate the service function "green" for effectiveness but "red" for cycle time. Even though specific category trends may reflect higher performance, the team may opt to show the lowest color rating classification.

8. Identify major types of resources (people, information technology, materials, equipment, facilities, and so on) required to perform the service activities identified in the enterprise map.

Tip Consider applying rating schemas at the resource level to give the enterprise mapping team and leadership clearer insight as to the strengths and weakness of a service process. Similar to the function level ratings, resource ratings can also be rated on effectiveness, efficiency, cycle time, integration, and total costs.

Tip
Consider adding commentary to the enterprise diagram to indicate rationale for ratings.

Tip
The goal is to diagram the enterprise map such that it does not exceed a single page. This page may be an engineering "E" size paper (34"x 44") or more common tabloid size (11"x17"). Make the document both useful in content and easy to read.

Tip
Given the holistic nature of an enterprise map, they are typically produced and disseminated in electronic media, such as Microsoft PowerPoint, Visio, Excel, AutoCAD, etc., with whole sections or individual functions hyperlinked to more detailed diagrams, metrics, and associated documents.

Example: SERV-ALL color coded (indicated by shading for the purposes of this illustration) its enterprise map based on both anecdotal and fact-based evidence. They chose a red, yellow, green rating schema as available data did not support a numerical rating scheme based on sigma levels. They rated not only the overall function but also the effectiveness of each of the resources used to complete the function. For example, Service Lanes were rated red because the operating procedures were unclear, facilities inadequate, and material quality poor. This was the first area addressed by the SERV-ALL lean activities.

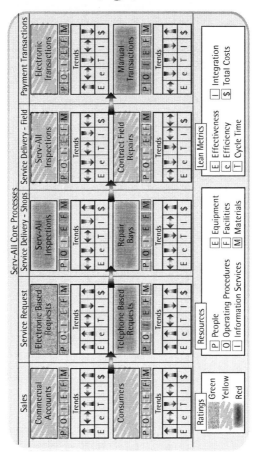

9. Identify the value streams to be analyzed. All value stream maps created by an organization should support or integrate with the enterprise map or an extended enterprise map. Your organization may assign various value streams to different teams, with the caveat that results are integrated so that the enterprise benefits from the independent efforts. The goal is to avoid suboptimization of processes within and between departments and/or operations.

 Example: From their enterprise map analysis, SERV-ALL leadership determined that its lean enterprise initiative should focus on achieving continuous flow through its shop services to include the processes of materials management, facility management, contract management, fleet management, information services, and work methods. It surmised that its information systems, where highly disintegrated (customer profiles, service scheduling, equipment identification and servicing, through billing and payment receipt), added to inefficient and costly practices. Furthermore, SERV-ALL surmised that its material acquisition, stocking, issuing, and replenishment practices negatively affected its ability to conduct repairs correctly the first time and extended cycle time. Finally, it stated that its shop organization and fleet capabilities did not match the nature of the services they were performing.

Often a service improvement opportunity touches upon many facets of an organization—

with not all knowing or believing that a performance problem exists! Don't be overwhelmed by the prospect of having to work across departments, challenging old ways of doing business, and potentially restructuring the way work is done. A lean initiative doesn't have to become a mean initiative if care is taken to understand how resources can be more effectively deployed to meet service demands. But lean gets mean when your organization doesn't effectively manage the change of the lean initiative. Chapter 2, "Lean Leadership," has additional tips for managing the change process.

10. Map the future state enterprise map. Now is the time to begin mapping how you would like things to be done. The development of a future state enterprise map is a relatively straight-forward process. It begins by identifying the activities that require strengthening based on current ratings and the availability of solutions (information technology, work flows and methods, decision protocols, facilities, equipment, organization structures, and so on). Once identified, the enterprise map provides the basis for valuing and ranking improvement initiatives.

Ultimately the enterprise map drives the development of functional requirements for resources such as new information technology, work methods, required skills, and so on. In simple terms, functional requirements define what a resource should be able to do and the functions it should be capable of performing.

Serv-All "Future State" Service Lane Map
Functional Requirements and Projected Ratings

Sales	Service Request

Commercial Accounts

`P` `O` `I` `E` `F` `M` ➡➡

Trends

⬆	↔	⬆	↔	⬆
E	e	T	I	$

Electronic Based Requests

`P` `O` `I` `E` `F` `M` ➡

continued on next page

Trends

⬆	↔	⬆	⬇	⬆
E	e	T	I	$

Functional Requirements

Develop sales communication offering new service process

- define service features
- communicate benefits
- detail scheduling process
- provide point of contact for consumer questions

Modify sales incentive program

Functional Requirements

Web-based scheduling application

- integrate with current business system
- establish templates for standard services
- communicates standard services provided by Serv-All's service lanes
- provide ability to modify schedules
- provide automated alerts to schedule changes

Ratings

- Green
- Yellow
- Red

Lean Metrics

`E` Effectiveness	`I` Integration
`e` Efficiency	`$` Total Costs
`T` Cycle Time	

Resources

`P` People	`E` Equipment
`O` Operating Procedures	`F` Facilities
`I` Information Services	`M` Materials

Serv-All "Future State" Continued

Service Delivery - Shops	Payment Transactions

Functional Requirements	Functional Requirements
• develop continuous flow value stream map • apply queue analysis • apply visual management • apply quick changeover • apply error proofing • apply standard operations • apply kanban to material replenishment	• accept electronic payment information to reserve time in queue • indicate potential cost penalties for missing appointment and late arrivals

Example: SERV-ALL developed functional requirements for its shop services—requirements such as providing walk-in service for consumers based on a First In First Out (FIFO) queue. Furthermore, they desired that customers schedule their arrival time based on available time slots using a web-based scheduling system. If a customer were to walk in without prior notice, this same system would be used to slot customers in to the service queue, thus enabling the SERV-ALL service desk to give customers feedback as to the likely time that service would be performed. Customers can opt to wait or come back.

Functional requirements obtained through the enterprise mapping activity drive design requirements for the specific changes an organization must conduct in order to achieve lean practices, such as continuous flow, quick changeover, error proofing, visual management, and so on.

 The future state enterprise map will provide guidance to value stream mapping teams to drive local improvements that benefit the entire enterprise.

 Often the future state enterprise map appears to supersede the need to develop a "current state" value stream map as organizations jump to conclusions. Just be cautious in executing lean changes that leave people bewildered about what is happening, not understanding the need for change, and with little understanding of how the change will be implemented. A quick mapping of current practices might be what is needed to gain support for a bigger change.

 Do not lock in your future state enterprise map until it has been validated against the principles and practices of a lean enterprise contained in this pocket guide.

VALUE STREAM MAPPING

The analysis of the map consists of identifying the various ways in which the lean principles can be applied. These are likely to include:

- ◻ Moving from a push to a pull process
- ◻ Reducing batching
- ◻ Balancing the capacity of the different stages of the process
- ◻ Eliminating non-value-adding steps
- ◻ Moving decision points earlier in the process
- ◻ Simplifying individual steps
- ◻ Reducing the cycle times or changeover times of individual steps
- ◻ Improving the flow of information between steps

What Is a Value Stream?

The term value stream refers to all the activities your company must do to deliver its services to internal or external customers. A value stream has four main parts:

1. The flow of activities, from the initial determination of customer need to the delivery of the service through the completion of associated transactions.

2. The identification of resources (people, information technology, materials, equipment, facilities, instructions) required for service delivery and transaction completion.

3. The transformation of data into information for guiding and improving value stream activities.

4. The classification of activities as value-adding or non-value-adding and their associated lead times.

There are often several value streams operating within a company, as demonstrated in an enterprise map; value streams can also involve more than one company.

What Is a Value Stream Map and What Does It Do?

A value stream map uses simple graphics or icons to show the sequence of activities, the flow of information, the identification and alignment of resources,

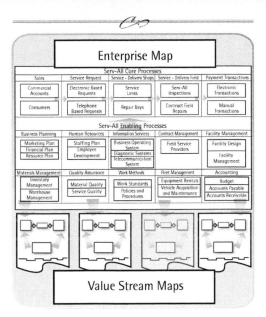

Enterprise Map

Serv-All Core Processes

Sales	Service Request	Service - Delivery Shops	Service - Delivery Field	Payment Transactions
Commercial Accounts	Electronic Based Requests	Service Lanes	Serv-All Inspections	Electronic Transactions
Consumers	Telephone Based Requests	Repair Bays	Contract Field Repairs	Manual Transactions

Serv-All Enabling Processes

Business Planning	Human Resources	Information Services	Contract Management	Facility Management
Marketing Plan / Financial Plan / Resource Plan	Staffing Plan / Employee Development	Business Operating System / Diagnostic Systems / Telecommunication System	Field Service Providers	Facility Design / Facility Management

Materials Management	Quality Assurance	Work Methods	Fleet Management	Accounting
Inventory Management / Warehouse Management	Material Quality / Service Quality	Work Standards / Policies and Procedures	Equipment Rentals / Vehicle Acquisition and Maintenance	Budget / Accounts Payable / Accounts Receivable

Value Stream Maps

the identification of value creation and value destruction (waste), and the lead time of specific value stream activities.

It helps employees understand the complexities of services—that they often require more input and resources than imagined and that waste can sneak into virtually all aspects of their delivery.

Why use it?

Once you have framed potential lean activities through the development and analysis of an enterprise map, creation of the value stream map is the next step your company should take in executing a specific lean-initiative plan. A lean initiative begins with agreement among employees that an improved future state is worth the investment in time and resources to achieve it. Ideally, the enterprise map begins this process (Chapter 3). Many organizations begin the process at a more tactical level and simply desire to eliminate waste as part of a continuous improvement effort. In this case a value stream map of the current state of your organization is the logical place to start. In either case, developing a visual map of the value stream allows everyone to fully understand and agree on how value is produced and where waste occurs. Creating a value stream map also provides these benefits:

- ◻ Highlights the connections among activities, resources, and information that affect the value creation and lead time of your company's value stream.

- ◻ Helps employees understand your services' entire value stream rather than just a single activity or transaction associated with it.

- ◻ Improves the decision-making process of all work teams by helping team members to understand and accept your company's current service practices and future plans.

◻ Creates a common visualization, language, and
  understanding of activities among employees
  through the use of standard value-stream-map-
  ping symbols.

◻ Allows you to separate value-creating activities
  from value-destroying activities and then evaluate their impact on lead time.

◻ Provides a way for employees to easily identify
  and plan for the elimination of waste.

What areas should I focus on to create a value stream map?

To create an effective value stream map for
your company's service offerings or processes, you
should focus on these areas:

◻ *The flow of service activities,* from the identification of
  a customer need through design, service delivery,
  and completion of all associated transactions.
  Activities are things one does. Activities have
  outputs that serve as inputs to downstream
  activities and require inputs from upstream
  activities, thus, the concept of service flow.

◻ *Service demand characteristics,* often random, sporadic, and unpredictable, making value stream
  optimization of a service process a unique
  challenge.

□ **Resource alignment,** which is the identification of all resources (people, information technology, equipment, facilities, materials) required to accomplish service activities.

□ **Information flow,** which includes the initial gathering of data, transforming it into useful information, deploying it through various mediums, and ultimately using it to evaluate and improve service performance.

□ **Customer value,** which is an aspect of a service delivery for which a customer is willing to pay. (This is sometimes referred to as value added or value creation.)

□ A *push system,* where service resources are automatically made available, whether or not they are needed.

□ A *pull system,* where services are delivered at the time of need and service resources are made available based on service delivery timing requirements and in the desired sequence (queue), but not before.

□ **Queuing strategy,** where several related processes or work activities are sequenced, to include arriving at the (back of the) queue, waiting in the queue (essentially a storage process), and being served by the server(s) at the front of the queue.

□ **Waste, non-value-adding, or value-destroying activities** involved in your service processes.

- **Takt time,** which is the amount of available time your employees have to conduct an aspect of a service, divided by the rate of customer demand. Takt time sets the pace of service delivery to match the rate of customer demand.

- **Lead time,** which is the time it takes to complete an activity from start to finish. Lead time contains activity cycle time, batch, and process delays.

- **Time standard,** the estimated or derived average time to conduct service activities, used in queuing strategies and scheduling systems.

- Finally, you need to become familiar with the following four types of icons, which are described in detail later in this chapter:

    - Activity flow icons

    - Information flow icons

    - Resource icons

    - Lean Enterprise icons

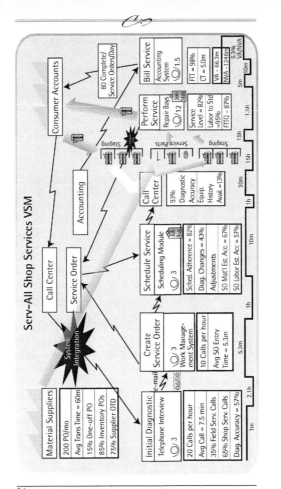

Serv-All Shop Services VSM

How do I create a value stream map?

To begin, all employees should map the value stream on their own. Usually, each employee's map will be different from all the others. Then, by comparing maps and working together to reach a consensus, your work team can develop the most accurate map of the value stream possible.

▫ Select a service or service grouping to map. You should conduct a process quantity (P_cQ) analysis (Chapter 5) to determine what the major service groupings or cluster of offerings are before you map the dominant service offerings value stream.

▫ Assemble paper, pencils, erasers, and a stopwatch to use when collecting data.

▫ Conduct a quick physical or virtual tour of the value stream to view the end-to-end service process, resources, and information flows, making sure that you have identified all the activities.

 Don't work from memory. Observe the value stream in action. Interview team members from different shifts and similar service operations, if applicable. Verify your observations against documented policies, procedures, work flows, and job aids.

If the service requires the use of software applications, perform sequential screen captures to document the flow of tasks and information.

 Remember to record exactly what you see without making any judgments. There is no right or wrong. Don't waste time debating the merits of an activity or its proper sequence; just record what is actually happening. Evaluation will come later.

❑ From the P$_c$Q analysis identify a representative customer of the service under review. Once you have identified a typical customer, gather data about typical types of services acquired, demand drivers, information flow, timing, frequencies, and associated transactions. This information will help you establish the takt time for the customer and associated services.

 Don't be surprised if not enough data exist for you to accurately define the amount and frequency of services demanded by the customer. It is common for certain services to simply occur both randomly and infrequently. If this is the case, human judgment of demand patterns will often suffice if the number of service offerings is relatively small.

❑ Begin mapping the value stream, starting with customer requirements and going through the major service activities. Document the value stream just as it is. The result is a current state map of the value stream.

Begin mapping the value stream using Post-it Notes, which can be easily rearranged while your team comes to a consensus, or use a pencil and eraser to draw and refine your map. Add activity-flow, information-flow, resource icons, and lean enterprise icons (see page 60 for details on these icons) to your value stream map.

During data collection, show whether information is communicated in real time or in batches, or if it requires multiple resources to review. If it is communicated in batches, show the size of the batches, how often they are sent, and the average time of the batch delay. If the information must be reviewed by multiple resources, indicate average process delays.

Identify every location where service work is backlogged. For example, outstanding service requests or work orders are referred to as a backlog of work to be scheduled or placed in a queue. This backlog is equivalent to an inventory of work. The capacity and rate at which a company performs current service requirements and clears its backlog of work is dependent both on the nature of the service and the combination of resources needed for its performance.

Identify all value-creating and value-destroying activities in all the service, resource, and information flows.

◻ Create a lead time chart at the bottom of your value stream map, showing the value-creating and value-destroying activity lead times.

◻ Review the map with all the employees who work in the value stream you have mapped to ensure that you haven't missed any service activities and associated transactions.

Sample Activity Flow Icons

◻ **Service activity.** The top of the icon shows the name of the service or service group being mapped. The bottom of the icon shows resources, information, or a relevant lean-enterprise technique.

Schedule Work
Scheduling Module
◯/ 3

Call Center

◻ **Outside sources.** These include customers and suppliers. Try to use typical customers or suppliers for your mapping activities.

Consumer Accounts

Material Suppliers

◻ **Data box.** This is a place for key data such as

200 PO/mo
Avg Trans Time = 60m
15% One-off PO
85% Inventory POs
75% Supplier OTD

20 Calls per hour
Avg Call = 7.5 min
35% Field Serv. Calls
65% Shop Serv. Calls
Diag. Accuracy = 57%

service time standard; cycle time; number of service variations; whether service frequency occurs continu-

ously, hourly, daily, weekly; the number and types
of resources required; the service driver; capacity;
and first-time-through (FTT) quality levels. If the
service you are mapping requires significant use
of special equipment, consider recording the
equipment's performance level, using the Overall
Equipment Effectiveness (OEE) metric. If the
service is labor intensive consider measuring
performance using the Overall Labor Effectiveness
(OLE) metric. Lastly when mapping a service process identify the constraining operation or task.

◻ **People.** Shows the number of employees required
to perform an operation. "Partial people"
can be used; for example, 0.5 means that
an employee spends half of his or her time
performing a particular operation.

Sample Material Flow Icons

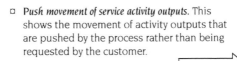

◻ **Push movement of service activity outputs.** This
shows the movement of activity outputs that
are pushed by the process rather than being
requested by the customer.

◻ **Pull movement of service activity
outputs.** This shows the movement of activity
outputs that are requested by the customer (i.e.,
they are not pushed).

◻ **Automated movement of activity outputs.** Indicates
that automation is used to move activity outputs from one process to another.

- □ **FIFO** *queue.* Indicates that services will be
  delivered on a first-in, first-out (FIFO)
  basis. Using this method, the oldest
  remaining items in a backlog of work are the
  first to move forward in the service delivery
  process.

- □ **Scheduled** *queue.* Indicates that services will be delivered on a scheduled
  basis. This method estimates service
  duration or preexisting time standards that are
  used to schedule service activities into available
  time slots.

- □ **Rail** *shipment.* Shows the movement of service
  materials, special equipment, tools,
  and so on, by train. Be sure to show the
  frequency of shipments on your map.

- □ **Truck** *shipment.* Shows the movement of service
  materials, special equipment, and
  tools by truck. Be sure to show the
  frequency of shipments on your map.

- □ **Air** *shipment.* Shows the movement of
  service materials, special equipment,
  and tools by plane. Be sure to show the
  frequency of shipments on your map.

- □ **Ship** *Movement.* Shows the movement of service
  materials, special equipment, and tools by ship
  or boat. Be sure to show the frequency of shipments on your map.

□ **Inventory.** Indicates the inventory of service materials, special equipment, and tools by count and supply remaining in time (e.g., there are two years of supply on hand).

30 parts

□ **Backlog.** Shows the backlog of service activities that remain to be performed by count and estimated time.

□ **Storage.** Shows all materials, special equipment, and tools needed to perform a service that can be contained in a storage area. You can note the average material investment, turnover, and service levels if so desired.

Sample Information Flow Icons

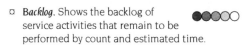

□ **Data input.** Manual input by a person into an information technology application.

□ **Data download.** Download of data from an information technology application.

□ **Data upload.** Upload of data from an information technology application.

□ **Manual information flow.** Shows information that is transferred by hand.

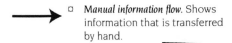

□ **Electronic information flow.** Shows information that is transferred via computer.

□ **Information type.** Indicates the type of information being communicated.

□ **Service order.** A card used to initiate the service activity. (Used for service queuing or scheduling systems only; see Chapter 6, "Queuing Strategies," for details.)

□ **Material request.** A card used to obtain service materials, special equipment, or tools from a storage area. (Used for service queuing or scheduling systems only.)

□ **Service Order box.** Similar to a mailbox, this is used for the storage and retrieval of service orders. (Used for service queuing or scheduling systems only.)

□ **Service leveling.** Shows when resource leveling is used to even out the volume and mix of service activities.

OXOX

Sample Lean Manufacturing Icons

□ **Kaizen Burst (Continuous Improvement).** Shows the existence of waste or value-destroying activity.

□ **Visual management.** Shows that visual management techniques have been applied. (Chapter 7).

□ **Error proofing.** Shows that error-proofing techniques have been applied (Chapter 8).

□ *Quick changeover*. Indicates that quick changeover techniques (see *The Lean Enterprise Memory Jogger™ for Production*) have been applied.

 □ *Service standards*. Shows that your company's service standards are in place.

□ *Stretch objectives*. Shows where stretch objectives for fostering improvement have been set for specific operations or for the value stream as a whole.

□ *Performance boards*. Indicates that process objectives and results have been posted in an operation's work area.

□ *Constraining activity*. Shows which activity or activities constrain, or limit, the progress of the value stream.

How do I use my team's value stream map to make future improvements in my organization?

After your team completes a map showing your organization's value stream in its current state, what's next? First, familiarize yourself with the lean methods and tools outlined in this book. Then consider the ideas below as you review your value stream map to plan future improvements for your organization.

Understand Service Demand

The first premise of optimizing a value stream is simple: _Supply must deliver to demand and only to demand at the time of demand, in the quality and quantity demanded._ But what if demand is a constantly moving target in terms of timing, quantity, and variation of output?

Lean separates itself from other performance improvement methodologies in that it also attempts to optimize supply in terms of the resources (people, technology, equipment, tools, and so on), instruction (method, order of work), and aggregation of work (batch or continuous flow) it takes to deliver the service.

When one attempts to standardize the output of supply in the face of a constantly moving demand target (type, time, and quantity) one will find gross over- and underperformance.

We all face this challenge and lean methodologies do lead us to a solution. However, the traditional manufacturing application of lean should not be applied to service wholesale…without thinking first!

Start your future state value stream map with a demand analysis using the P_cQ analysis. Leading practitioners have transitioned the product quantity (PQ) analysis to process quantity (P_cQ) to understand the nature of demand for services. The P_cQ analysis will be discussed in Chapter 5, "Continuous Flow."

Look at Your Takt Time

The third lean goal is to match supply to demand (Chapter 1). An organization meets this goal by first having a clear understanding of the likely occurrence of demand. Does demand occur once, twice, or one hundred times a day? The customer owns the demand; your organization owns the supply. In the service world, where demand is often sporadic and the lead times for supply are short, takt time is the broadest estimate of how often supply of services must occur to meet an average demand level over a defined period of time.

Your goal is to get your organization's value stream to produce to the takt time. Be mindful that different service processes and offerings may have different demand rates as occurring different times of the day (inside and outside of your service window) and thus may have different takt times.

To calculate the takt time that your service processes must generally meet, use the following guideline:

takt time = *available daily service time*
(*i.e., hours of operations*)

required daily quantity of output
(*i.e., customer demand*)

Theoretically, when the value stream makes service resources available ahead of the takt time, over-capacity occurs; when it produces behind the takt time, undercapacity occurs.

For example, you perform services over an eight-hour period (480 minutes). You perform 200 service events in that period of time. Therefore, your takt time is 480 minutes/200 service events = 24 minutes. So every twenty-four minutes per service event, on average, you should deliver a service event such that supply matches demand.

In practice, organizations forecast the nature and timing of service demand based on historical trends or their projections of new demand. Because service demands are often out of your control—for example, they are controlled by the customer in both timing and variation—it's likely that takt time is an inappropriate strategy for basing resource capacity and scheduling. You may have one-half (in the example, 100) of the typical demands for service in the first two hours of the day and the rest spread out evenly throughout the rest of the day. Do you design service rules and capacity to level the load based on takt time when it may result in customer dissatisfaction? In this case, you may have multiple takt times based on service windows. Service industries must analyze demands to assemble resources in the right combination, capabilities, and capacity to deliver services at the right time.

Other terms, similar in intent, to takt time include mean time between service (MTBS), mean time between incident (MTBI), mean time between failure (MTBF), and mean time between transaction (MTBT). Organizations often use these statistics to forecast resource and capacity requirements. The challenge, however, is that a significant number of services can be characterized as sporadic and don't provide enough data upon which to accurately predict the next occurrence of the service need. Again, without delving too deeply in statistical methods, just know that human judgment of demand patterns will often suffice if the number of service offerings is relatively small.

Finally, consider the length of time it takes to perform defined services, by mean (average) and standard deviation (range), to estimate the time component of work standards. Use mean time between service events (MTBS, MTBI, MTBF, MTBT, etc.) in combination with work standards to assist your demand forecasting efforts.

Apply Continuous Flow Principles

Does your value stream have large backlogs of work and numerous delays associated with the most critical or highest-priority services? Such delays in performing services can occur because of their sporadic nature, disintegrated processing of information, not having all of the resources available at the right time, poor process designs, and so on. To eliminate wasteful delays, try applying continuous-flow principles to your value stream (Chapter 4).

Apply Quick-Change, Error Proofing, and Visual Management Techniques

□ Can you use quick-change methods to increase your ability to quickly and efficiently deliver multiple services or variants thereof using similar or different resources? (See *The Lean Enterprise Memory Jogger™ for Production*.) By reducing changeover times, your company will be able to perform more services and free up resource capacity. If being able to offer a mix of services is important, then quick changeover will help you rethink how to reduce costly resource delays.

□ Can you use error proofing techniques to ensure that no service or transactional defects are being passed on to downstream activities or to your customer? (Chapter 8) As service variations become larger and resources are called upon to do multiple tasks in shorter cycle times, with shorter lead times between services, the impact of defects on your service delivery increases. This is especially true if defects shut down your operations or harm your customer.

▫ Have you conducted visual management activities, such as the 5 S's (sort, shine, set in order, standardize, and sustain), in your important service work or delivery areas? (Chapter 7) A well-organized and well-maintained workplace is key to ensuring that all employees perform their duties correctly, safely, and in a proper manner, all of which ensures quality results.

Apply Work-Standardization Techniques

Have you developed work standards to estimate service work in order to improve planning and scheduling activities? Have you compared them to actual times and resources to improve their accuracy? Are these work standards readily available in various media to support service delivery? Are they easy to understand? Do they reflect current practices? Are they reviewed to ensure they reduce or eliminate waste?

Use Service Leveling

▫ After applying continuous flow, quick-changeover, error proofing, visual management, and work-standardization techniques, try using service leveling in your value stream. This prevents overcapacity and undercapacity of service resources during expected periods of demand.

- ◻ For example, even as unplanned services increase based on new customer demand, you still must perform planned work to meet compliance requirements. Employing service leveling practices would mean moving activities up and down the queue to match resources to priorities within a given time period.

◻ Check your service sequence. This can have a significant effect on your ability to perform multiple, repeat, or different services to more efficiently meet customer requirements. Sequencing includes the services as a complete process as well as the individual steps within a service process.

- ◻ For example, when a service provider must go to the customer, planning activities must take into account kitting materials and the time needed to organize them based on their sequence of use. In addition, delivery routes should be devised to best sequence the order of service delivery to minimize travel time.

- ◻ Or, when the customer comes to the service provider, they must sequence service based on resource capability and availability. When all demands are equivalent in importance and capable resources are available, a first-come, first-serve strategy might be employed. When demands have varying levels of importance, or resources to complete the service are limited, sequencing may be based on service priorities (Chapter 6).

Establish Lean Metrics

Establish metrics for your value stream to make sure that you are meeting lead time, waste-reduction, and cost objectives. Chapter 10, "Lean Metrics," provides an introduction to core-process measures that you can apply to your organization's value stream.

Use Other Tools to Complement Your Value Stream Map

You can obtain excellent insight into your organization's current and future operational practices by using a value stream map in conjunction with flowcharts (see *The Problem Solving Memory Jogger™* for details) and a workflow diagram (Chapter 9).

Because the map provides you with a "big picture" view of several linked service activities, it's a good starting point. You can then describe the details of specific processes using flowcharting techniques.

A process route diagram is an excellent tool for understanding common activities between multiple service offerings. It offers insight into potential aggregation and sequencing of activities. It helps an organization define capability requirements that may narrow or stretch work requirements.

A workflow diagram is useful for gathering physical information, such as the distance between work activities and the movement of employees and materials. It is possible to record information on a value stream map, but it's easily understood on a workflow diagram.

In combination, the process quantity (P_cQ) analysis, process route, process capacity, standard operations combination chart, and process flow diagrams aid in the application of continuous flow resource efficiencies.

CONTINUOUS FLOW

Imagine streams of activities each flowing into each other, effortlessly, without interruption, with a constant movement as if drawn by a purpose greater than them. Imagine these streams widening or narrowing, raising or lowering, accelerating or slowing, depending on the magnitude and urgency of the need...Imagine continuous flow with a mission.

What Is Continuous Flow?

Continuous flow is the sequencing of activities through the entire service process, one task "unit of work" at a time, to minimize delays and reduce the overall lead time. This is in contrast to batch processing, which creates batch delays when similar work is grouped for completion. Continuous flow is also compared and contrasted to work flow, where service tasks flow from one responsible person or department to another, and where process delays occur as tasks wait in a queue in the downstream operation.

 For example, SERV-ALL's Call Center enters multiple field service requests before they e-mail any of these requests to a service center, thus creating batch delays. The service center planner only processes new service requests twice per day, thus creating process delays. In a continuous flow operation, the service request would flow immediately via integrated technology from the call center to the service center planner, who would begin processing immediately.

Continuous flow focuses employees' efforts on conducting the service process itself rather than on waiting for input, searching for resources, and creating significant backlogs of work. It also makes the service process flow smoothly, one task at a time, creating a steady, efficient, and timely workload for all employees involved.

Why use it?

There are many advantages to incorporating the continuous flow method into your work processes, including the following:

▢ It reduces the time that elapses between a customer need and the service delivery.

□ It prevents the wait times that can result from batch and process delays.

□ By reducing excess backlog of work, it reduces wasteful investment in resources such as labor, facilities, special equipment, materials, and tools.

□ It reveals any problems early in service delivery process.

□ It provides both speed and adaptability in service queuing and routing systems.

□ It reduces your operating costs by making value-destroying work more evident, thus eliminating waste.

□ It gives your organization the greatest flexibility to meet customer demand at the time of demand, the first time, every time, and at the lowest cost.

Example: SERV-ALL Implements Continuous Flow

 SERV-ALL is a hypothetical company that responds to customer demands for repair services. The repair service process involves nine basic activities, as shown in the table below.

Each of these nine activities requires different capabilities and resources and each has varying lead times based on the nature of the service call. Let's briefly review high-level tasks performed by each activity.

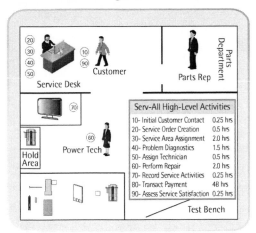

Serv-All High-Level Activities

Activity	Time
10- Initial Customer Contact	0.25 hrs
20- Service Order Creation	0.5 hrs
30- Service Area Assignment	2.0 hrs
40- Problem Diagnostics	1.5 hrs
50- Assign Technician	0.5 hrs
60- Perform Repair	2.0 hrs
70- Record Service Activities	0.25 hrs
80- Transact Payment	48 hrs
90- Assess Service Satisfaction	0.25 hrs

Activity Tasks

10—Initial Customer Contact. The customer makes phone contact with SERV-ALL's contract call center and requests service center support. Typical lead time is 15 minutes.

20—Service Order Creation. The call center representative completes a service request form and e-mails it to one of three SERV-ALL's area repair centers based on predefined territories. The typical lead time for this activity is 30 minutes.

30—Service Area Assignment. The area repair center then contacts the customer to schedule an appointment or offer first-come, first-serve service, depending on the nature of the request. The lead time is typically 2 hours.

40—Problem Diagnostics. The repair center conducts an analysis to determine the potential causes of the service problem so that it can assign the right resource capabilities to solve it. The lead time is typically 1.5 hours.

50—Resource Assignment. The repair center has two main service areas: the FCFS (First-Come, First-Serve), which is a First In First Out (FIFO) Queue, and BAO (By Appointment Only). If a service window opens up in the BAO area, a select FCFS work service is slotted into that window. The lead time for assignment of resources is 30 minutes.

60—Perform Repair. SERV-ALL resources must follow repair standards, using safe practices, preferred materials, and qualified personnel. These resources do not always come together at the time of need. Even scheduled work may be delayed as the repair process uncovers new or unexpected problems. The typical lead time for repair activities is 2 hours.

70—Record Activities. SERV-ALL requires that accurate records of the problem, cause, and remedy be kept. It also requires that labor type and hours, repair materials, and any special equipment used be recorded. The average lead time for these activities is 15 minutes.

80—Transact Payment. SERV-ALL accepts multiple payment types: cash, check, credit card, and purchase orders from commercial accounts. Average lead time for check or credit card payments is 2 days. SERV-ALL typically processes between 25 and 125 payments per day.

90—Assess Service Satisfaction. SERV-ALL provides its customers with hard copy satisfaction surveys upon the completion of all repairs. These can be mailed in or given to a service representative. SERV-ALL also samples recent customers with follow-up satisfaction phone calls. The average lead time for this activity is 15 minutes.

What is not readily apparent in these nine activities is the long delay that exists between each activity, as well as within certain activities. For example, the call center is only open for nine hours each day. It may take an additional twelve hours before the SERV-ALL repair center is actually notified that a service need exists. SERV-ALL works overtime for approved priority work, but a backlog of work is commonplace as service orders wait on materials, labor, and equipment availability. Customers waiting for FCFS repairs often spend their day in the customer lounge.

SERV-ALL's Lead Time Bottom Line

What appears to be a straightforward seven hours from time of need to completion of the service work may, in fact, be closer to 168 hours!

In a continuous flow process, as soon as one task is finished, the next is immediately started, and so on until all activities are completed. Continuous flow

Current State Value Stream Map → ... → Updated Value Stream Map

Evaluate Current Conditions	Determine Suitability for Flow	Develop Flow Concepts	Identify Flow Inhibitors/Enablers	Validate and Improve Flow	Standardize Operations
Product or Process Quantity Analysis ($P_Q Q$)	Product/ Service Groupings	Physical Layouts and Flow – (PF)	Develop Future State Value Stream Map	Create Flow Implementation Plan	Develop Standard Operating Procedures
Process Route Analysis (PR)	Drivers	Virtual "Information" Flow	Identify Wastes & Apply Lean Solutions	Conduct Trial Run and Validate Flow	Monitor and Improve Workforce Capabilities
Process Flow Diagram (PF)	Requirements	Estimate New Cycle Times (SOCC)	Multifunction & Right Sized Resources	Update Lean Analysis Documents	Monitor and Improve Flow
Standard Operations Combination Chart (SOCC)		Balance Activities – (SOCC)	Multiskilled Workforce	Establish New Work Environment	

would enable SERV-ALL to significantly reduce its overall lead time. How much? Real-world service operations benchmark lead times for both value creating and value-destroying activities, through the use of value stream maps. By reducing or eliminating waste, it is not uncommon to see 50% or greater improvement in lead times in the service environment.

How do I do it?

This pocket guide contains advice and tools for helping your organization apply continuous flow—in cases where it makes sense to do so! To help your decision making and continuous flow transformation activities consider this six phase approach.

Phase 1: Evaluate Current Condition

During this phase your lean team will use tools to help you best describe both the demand and supply characteristics of your service processes. Input from the value stream map of current practices is used to apply these tools:

P_cQ *analysis:* The P_c stands for process/service type; the Q stands for quantity of output. This tool helps employees understand the types of products and services produced and the volume that the customers demand. It also shows whether most of the products/services are made up of a small or wide variety of offerings, thus helping employees identify what products are suitable for continuous flow.

Process route analysis: This table shows the resources required for conducting the tasks in the operation. Such a table helps to arrange resources in process lines according to process/service type and group-related tasks, creating well-crafted physical and virtual workflows. Swim-lane and deployment charts are variants of the process route analysis; just be mindful that the purpose of the process route analysis is to look for which services and associated resources can be grouped for improved flow. Charting a single service will be insufficient for this analysis.

Process flow diagram: This standard operation chart allows analysis of the work sequence and the current operation layout. It also enables you to track the physical distances in which people and materials cross in order to complete a task. A "spaghetti diagram" is a popular version of a process flow diagram.

Standard operation combination chart: This study involves observing the tasks, recording them in the sequence in which they occur, and recording the associated time they take to complete, broken down by categories of manual, automated, walk, and wait.

Phase 2: Determine Suitability for Continuous Flow

To be clear, not all service processes can be designed or should be designed to achieve continuous flow. Depending on the availability of resources and flexibility of tools, materials, and equipment to be quickly and efficiently changed or substituted, achieving continuous flow may not be practical or cost effective for your company or service. However, in all cases, analyzing service processes with the goal of achieving continuous flow is a smart practice.

Offerings/service grouping. Group products or services so that tasks can be organized to maximize the available resources, while meeting customer requirements. To identify potential offerings/service groups, review P_cQ, PR, and SOCC analyses to determine:

◻ What offerings/services are delivered frequently to infrequently

◻ What offerings/services go through similar activities to be delivered

◻ What offerings/service lead times are required to meet customer requirements

Determine Continuous Flow Drivers

Align product/service delivery times with customer demand. After you really understand your services, answer these questions: Do demand requirements vary significantly by service offerings? Which services can we more directly match supply to demand—by how often and when?

Use a pull system to drive continuous flow activities. Can service delivery and associated resources be engaged or scheduled based on the occurrence of the customer demand?

Assess Requirements Applying Continuous Flow Methods

Must Haves. Continuous flow works when your service processes meet these requirements:

- ❏ Activities can be sequenced in a natural flow.

- ❏ Activity tasks are correctly sized to meet customer demand, one at a time. The process route diagram is an effective analysis technique for reviewing task size (by type of task, capability, and capacity requirements) and possibly for sequencing to achieve continuous flow.

- ❏ Resources (people, materials, facilities, equipment, tools, technology, etc.) can be made readily available at the time of need and sequenced to the work flow.

- ❏ Information systems are well-suited for achieving continuous flow. By default, system integration, i.e., enabling multiple applications to communicate and share data instantaneously, eliminates information batch delays. Most integrated systems also have work flow capability, which automatically routes information through the various steps of an activity. Appropriate work flows reduce lead time delays associated with process delays, such as awaiting approvals.

Nice to Haves. Continuous flow works best when your service processes can also meet these requirements:

- ❏ Multifunction resources, like information technology, facilities, equipment, can be used to conduct multiple required tasks, thus minimizing delays between tasks.

◻ Your company has a multi skilled workforce with the capability to perform various tasks required to ensure continuous flow.

◻ Some activities can be broken down into smaller tasks, which have defined outputs and are required inputs to subsequent tasks. The tasks used for continuous flow must be easy to set up quickly so that they can produce a wide mix of products/services, as determined by the process route analysis.

Phase 3: Develop Flow Concepts

Physical layout and flows. The idea is to minimize or eliminate conveyance by lining up the operation according to the improved process sequence. For the most part, service "office" or "field" environments don't have the same physical flow of activities as production operations.

The most obvious exception is repair centers, which may look like diagnostics, disassembly, repair, and assembly operations. In the health care industry, the emergency room or operating room can be likened to a production environment. If your service operation "acts" like a production activity, consider the following:

◻ Select the best line according to space: straight line, L-shaped line, or U-shaped line. Typically, U-shaped layouts are better than straight lines, which might create waste by making service personnel walk farther when going back to the start of the process. In a U-shaped layout, more experienced workers can handle the first and last processes, which are now in close proximity. In the office environment, the U-shape cell is often referred to as the swivel chair circle. Finally, avoid the enclosed circle layout design, which can create processing islands.

▫ Lines should have start and end points that maximize resource utilization.

▫ Find ways to shorten the distance between processes.

▫ Use specialized and general-purpose lines to best match supply resources to demand.

▫ Employ subassembly lines to handle frequently performed tasks that feed other work streams.

Lean organizations have tackled workplace organization to support improved work efficiencies. Consider these general tenets of workplace organization.

▫ Keep all pathways in work areas clear; avoid creating workspaces that face one another (this causes distractions) or looking directly away from one another (this causes isolation).

▫ Make sure separate work processes that are dependent on each other are located as physically or virtually close together as possible.

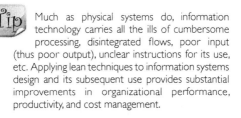

If you deliver your services at your customers' locations, consider how to apply continuous flow to service routes. Set up your service delivery routes to maximize employee productivity. Experts say that triangle shaped routes are the most efficient for servicing multiple locations and minimizing transit time.

Much as physical systems do, information technology carries all the ills of cumbersome processing, disintegrated flows, poor input (thus poor output), unclear instructions for its use, etc. Applying lean techniques to information systems design and its subsequent use provides substantial improvements in organizational performance, productivity, and cost management.

Consider these recommendations when applying continuous flow principles to information technology:

◻ **Information flows through distance.** Today's business applications and supporting information technology can make information available virtually anywhere in the world. What distances can be shortened through technology?

◻ **Information flows through time.** Data moves at near instantaneous speed to anywhere in the world; often this information must be stored or aggregated with other information for use in future applications. How can data be managed (formatted, validated, stored, retrieved) such that it provides "value in use" anytime that it is needed—now and into the future?

- ***Data is the raw material of information.*** How can we avoid "DRIP" (data rich, information poor) in other words, gathering data that has no real value or that is gathered in such a way that it diminishes its "value in use"? Data quality factors such as timeliness, accuracy, classification, segregation, and consistency will reduce the information "stops" and "stutters" associated with poor data inputs.

- ***Information is iterative.*** As data is raw material for information, similarly information is raw material for service activities. And like raw materials, information is put to its intended use, transformed, or put to some other purpose. Information technology now supports collaborative environments to rid the world of "over the wall" passing of information. Virtual data workbenches exist, where disparate participants can manage and modify information, as required, to create "value in use" without negatively affecting each other's core business systems.

- ***Information systems can bottleneck.*** Information bottlenecks inhibit the continuous flow of activities. For example, the physical or virtual pipelines by which information flows may not be large enough to process the data volume. Instability of an information pipeline can cause erratic and incomplete data transfers. Lost information can diminish productivity and drive up corporate risk. All of these might lead to either excess or underinvestment in technology to manage the flow of quality information.

◻ **Information flow can bottle neck.** Data may be held up or not entered into the system until a group of similar activities are completed—this is referred to as a batch delay. Information can also be held up between activities due to the timing of the next activity—this is referred to as a process delay.

Estimate New Cycle Times

Given the new process layout and sequence of work, rework the standard operations combination chart to estimate new cycle times.

Balance Activities

As a lean initiative pursues continuous flow, it is invariably challenged with how to define and organize tasks so that they do not constrain work flow, either upstream or downstream, from that activity. The use of the standard operations combination chart enables lean team members to break down functions by task (manual and automated) to determine if they can be rearranged, broken apart, or regrouped to achieve more balanced activities.

Phase 4: Identify Flow Inhibitors/Enablers

During this phase, your lean team will brainstorm known and predicted roadblocks to achieving continuous flow and their associated solutions.

- ❏ *Develop a future state value stream map.* Your lean team may have already developed a future state enterprise map; if not, now is the time to do so. If they have, now is the time to reevaluate its suitability for one-piece flow. Pay particular attention to defining:
    - ❏ Activities so that they flow.
    - ❏ Activities so that they are balanced.
    - ❏ Flow of resources (materials, tools, special equipment, etc.).
    - ❏ Information flow.
    - ❏ Job descriptions that support required tasks with minimum employee waste.
    - ❏ Equipment sizes, capability, capacity, etc., to support flow.

Identify Wastes and Apply Lean Solutions

Remember that wastes are activities that consume resources but create no value. There are eight types of waste:

- ❏ overservicing
- ❏ defects
- ❏ movement
- ❏ overprocessing

- ◻ transport

- ◻ waiting

- ◻ inventory

- ◻ lack of employee involvement and creativity.

These lean tools will help you identify and eliminate such wastes:

- ◻ value stream mapping

- ◻ visual management

- ◻ error proofing

- ◻ quick change

- ◻ standard operations

- ◻ lean metrics

Multifunction and Right-Sized Resources

Often, resources such as people, equipment, tools, materials, and information technology are instructed or designed to:

- ◻ Perform multiple functions although only one of them is primarily used.

- ◻ Perform a single function when multiple functions would reduce inputs, improve work flow, and reduce lead time.

Similarly, resources such as labor pool and equipment are sized (capacity and cycle time) to the following extremes:

- Perform a lot of work very quickly

- Perform a small amount of work very slowly

Multiskilled Workforce

Similar to multifunction and right-sized resources, human resource capabilities and their job responsibilities may have to change to support continuous flow designs. It is incorrect to assume that job responsibilities will expand to support continuous flow, although this is frequently thought to be the case. Where practical, cross-train employees so that they know how to perform multiple service tasks that might be required. This also enables an entire work team to take full responsibility for the service process.

 Make sure your lean team seeks input from Human Resources before roles and responsibilities are changed.

Phase 5: Validate and Improve Flow

During this phase, your team will develop a specific implementation plan that includes the testing, validation, and improvement of a trial continuous flow process.

Create flow implementation plan. Before your lean team begins its continuous flow transformation, it should develop an implementation plan. Consider the following major plan elements:

- ◻ Prepare the organization for change conditions.

- ◻ Conduct a trial run and validate activities.

- ◻ Update lean analysis documents.

- ◻ Establish the new work environment.

- ◻ Prepare the workforce for new roles and responsibilities.

- ◻ Establish standard operating procedures.

- ◻ Monitor and improve performance.

Conduct Trial Run and Validate Flow. A common mistake in attempting a conversion to continuous flow is a rush to implementation. This may result in disruptions to customer service, increased errors, employee disgruntlement, and so on. Be wise and conduct trial runs of new continuous flow activities. Bring key resources into the trial run. Gather feedback and measure results to drive improvements before you go "live" with the new workflow.

Establish the new work environment. Up to this point, the lean team has contemplated and tested new work flows. Now it's time to make it happen!

- ◻ Apply visual management and error proofing methodologies.

- ◻ Assemble necessary resources.

- ◻ Reset work environment.

- ◻ Create job aids.

- ◻ Create a feedback mechanism to support the change management process.

Phase 6: Standard Operations

During this phase, your lean team will establish the new work standards and protocols for operating and continually improving the new continuous flow process.

Develop standard operating procedures (SOPs). Now that you have the new continuous flow imagined and validated, and the new work environment established, it is time to update SOPs.

An excellent lean tool for capturing both work sequence and physical layouts is the standard operation sheet (SOS), which combines the best work sequence from a standard operations combination chart and the best physical workflow captured in a standard workflow diagram (SWD) (Chapter 9).

You should begin drafting new SOPs during the validation phase. Be sure everyone involved knows that the SOPs are *draft* only. First concentrate on the SOPs that support the new work flow.

Monitor and Improve Workforce Capabilities. Be prepared for confusion as both customers and employees experience the new workflow. Provide a mechanism to measure "How are we doing?" for customers and "How are you doing?" for employees. This is an essential step in a successful continuous flow transformation.

Monitor and improve flow. Be prepared for process hiccups such as insufficient resources and errors due to oversight. The lean team should imagine these potential problems when it prepares the continuous flow implementation plan. Now it's time to monitor and adjust the process to improve its performance.

Example:
SERV-ALL coordinates its cycle time with customer FCFS orders

SERV-ALL completed a P$_c$Q analysis of its service demand and decided to create two FCFS lines. Line two is dedicated to "designated work types," where customers can log on to the SERV-ALL web site or be processed by the call center and schedule service per available time slots. This process gives customers the ability to choose a service time that works for them and gives the SERV-ALL repair team plenty of time to stage potential parts and special equipment for the service. Line two FCFS is set up for customers who arrive unannounced but are given a time slot so they can plan the rest of their day. To balance the available work demands, FCFS associates are assigned to urgent scheduled work or to cover coworker time off.

Tip

Don't be tempted to create overcapacity with the goal of improving customer service levels, namely, adding extra resources (people, parts, equipment, tools) or extra shifts. This may simply cover up current process inefficiencies and wasteful practices. Improve planning activities, improve analysis techniques, align or stagger work hours to demand occurrence, and so on, but, first and foremost understand the nature of demand.

Example:
SERV-ALL deals with batch processes.

SERV-ALL followed its P_cQ (process quantity analysis) with a detailed process route (PR) analysis. It found numerous instances of batch processing that stifled the flow of information and repair activities. These included:

◻ Call center batching service requests to service center.

◻ Diagnostic department batching service orders to inspectors and, subsequently, to contract resources.

◻ Service technicians performing certain repair, overhaul, and upgrade activities in a batch mode.

◻ Service technicians returning completed service orders in batches.

SERV-ALL began its continuous flow activities by removing information batch delays between all entities involved in the service initiation and delivery process. This required investment in an information system that was directly accessible by all involved and integrated into the contractor work management systems. SERV-ALL developed business and functional information system requirements based on lean principles of continuous flow and waste elimination. For example, SERV-ALL's resulting system design enables the contract call center to view, assign, and modify service center schedules based on customer requirements. The call center can also track the status of mobile service resources, providing early notification capabilities to customers regarding schedule confirmations or disruptions. This ensures customer presence during the service delivery.

The service initiation system design also enables customers to enter service requests via SERV-ALL's web site—anytime they desire. This web access enables customers to select routine services and set service center appointments or request mobile service per a desired timeframe.

 ## Continuous Flow Tools

What tools should I be familiar with to implement a continuous-flow process?

Six tools are necessary to assess and plan for a continuous-flow process:

1. P$_c$Q analysis table

2. Process route diagram

3. Process capacity table

4. Standard operations combination chart

5. Standard workflow diagram

6. Standard operation sheet

P_cQ (Process Quantity) Analysis Table

A P_cQ analysis table is a tool that helps employees understand the types of services your organization delivers and the volume that your customers demand. In essence, it is a special application of the Pareto Analysis. It may also show whether the majority of your services are made up of a small or wide variety of offerings.

The P_cQ analysis table enables employees to identify what products are suitable for continuous flow production. (The P_c in P_cQ stands for a description of the service process; the Q stands for quantity of service output.)

Example: SERV-ALL P_cQ analysis

SERV-ALL conducted a P_cQ analysis of its repair services to see if a wide or limited variety of service offerings makes up most of the volume. P_cQ analyses were performed for mobile services as well as for service center services. The FCFS service processes identified on the next page are likely candidates for continuous flow operations.

P$_c$Q Analysis

Rank	Service Type	Quantity	Cumulative Total	%	Cumulative %
1	System Reset	375	1498	25.0%	25%
2	Circuit Board Replacement	225	600	15.0%	40.0%
3	6 mo. Warranty Inspection	180	780	12.0%	52.0%
4	Filter Replacement	150	930	10.0%	62.0%
5	Cable Replacement	135	1065	9.0%	71.0%
6	12 mo. Warranty Inspection	75	1140	5.0%	76.0%
7	Power System Repair	45	1185	3.0%	79.0%
8	Heat Sensor Replacement	15	1200	1.0%	80.0%
51	...	1	1497	0.1%	99.7%
52	...	1	1498	0.1%	99.8%
53	...	1	1499	0.1%	99.9%
	Total		1500		100.0%

Once the SERV-ALL team identified these services in a P$_c$Q analysis table, they created a process route table to determine whether similar resources (people, information technology, instruction, equipment, tools) are used to perform all FCFS repair services.

What is a process route diagram, and how do I use one?

A process route diagram shows what sequence and tasks are required for conducting a service process. Such a diagram helps you arrange your activities in process lines according to service type and, ultimately, to group related tasks into well-crafted physical and virtual workflows.

These are the steps for creating a process route table:

1. In the spaces across the top of the table, write the following:

    ▫ The name or number of the department whose service activities are being analyzed.

    ▫ The services that are being analyzed.

    ▫ The name of the person completing the form.

    ▫ The date on which the form is completed.

2. Use the "No." column on the left for the sequential numbering of the service tasks being analyzed according to ranked results from the P_cQ analysis.

3. For each service you are analyzing, enter its name.

4. Enter the common descriptions of tasks that each service must go through across the top of the diagram. Break apart tasks by major activity, not by who performs them. For example,

Serv-All Process Route

Department	
Service Centers	All
Service/Product	All
Data Collected by:	J. Smith
Data Collected on:	Aug 18th

Service Activity

No.	Service Type – Description	Disassemble System	Disassemble Components	Visual Inspection System	Visual Inspection Components	Clean System	Clean Components	Advanced Diagnostics System	Advanced Diagnostics Components	Repair Components	Replace Components	Assemble System	Assemble Components	Final Test System	Final Test Components
1	System Reset	1						2							
2	Circuit Board Replacement	1			2	3		4	5	9	6	7		8	9
3	6 mo. Warranty Inspection	1		2	3	4	5	6				7			8
4	Filter Replacement	1	2			3					4	5			
5	Cable Replacement	1	2		3		5		4		6	7	8		9
6	12 mo. Warranty Inspection	1		2	3	4	5	6			7			8	9
7	Power System Repair	1	2	3	4	5	6	7	8	9	10	11	12	13	14
8	Heat Sensor Replacement	1			2	3					4	5			

SERV-ALL's dissemble and inspection tasks are currently performed by one person. Do not group these activities; in the future these tasks may be assigned to different resources.

5. For each task, enter circled numbers in the various resource columns that correspond to the sequence in which the resources are used for that service.

6. Connect the circled numbers with lines or arrows to indicate the sequence of activities.

Once you have completed the table, look for services that follow the same, or nearly the same, sequence of tasks. You might be able to group these tasks and/ or resources together in the same physical or virtual workflow to improve the efficiency of your activities. See next page for detailed process route.

 For a more analytical analysis of the process route diagram, consider using a spreadsheet to combine results from demand analysis, lead-time analysis and task commonality analysis to quantify how frequently, for how long, and how commonly these tasks are performed. This will help in forming natural groupings of services and associated tasks.

Serv-All Process Route – Natural Groupings

Department	Service Centers
Service/Product	All
Data Collected by:	J. Smith
Data Collected on:	Aug 18th

No.	Description	Disassemble		Visual Inspection		Clean		Advanced Diagnostics		Repair	Replace	Assemble		Final Test	
		System	Components	System	Components	System	Components	System	Components	Components	Components	System	Components	System	Components
1	Power System Repair	1	2	3	4	5	6	7	8	9	10	11	12	13	14
2	Circuit Board Replacement	1			2	3		4	5		6	7		8	9
3	Cable Replacement	1	2		3	4	5				6	7	8		9
4	6 mo. Warranty Inspection	1		2	3	4	5	6				7			8
5	12 mo. Warranty Inspection	1		2	3	4	5	6			7			8	9
6	Filter Replacement	1			2	3					4	5			
7	Heat Sensor Replacement	1			2	3					4	6			
8	System Reset					1									2

Grouped Service Activities

What are the final steps?

Once services and tasks have been regrouped to improve resource utilization, apply continuous flow criteria to determine which groupings are likely candidates for improvement. Once selected, consider creating a standard operations combination chart. This chart enables you to study the task sequence for all your organization's service processes. In such a chart, each task is listed sequentially and then broken down into manual, automated, wait, and walk times. (See Chapter 9, "Standard Operations," for details about creating a standard operations combination chart.)

Next you should create a standard workflow diagram, which shows your organization's current work area layout and the movement of resources and workers during your service processes. It helps you identify areas of waste and plan improvements to your work layouts that will enable you to implement continuous flow production. (See Chapter 9, "Standard Operations," for details about creating a workflow diagram.)

Finally, your team should combine outputs from the standard operations combination chart with the standard workflow diagram to create a standard operations sheet. (See Chapter 9 for details about creating a standard operations sheet.) Once your work team collects all the data necessary for selecting the services that are suitable for continuous flow; verifies the resources needed and the available capacity; and understands the specific task in detail, you can implement the physical and/or virtual layout of your improved work processes and make continuous flow a reality in your organization.

QUEUING STRATEGIES

Quite simply, queuing strategies are sequencing techniques used to analyze and subsequently match service resources, in terms of capability, capacity, and timing to demand requirements of the customer.

What Are They?

Queuing strategies, when applied to service delivery, include sequencing of effort dimensions, which will be discussed in this section. Basic dimensions include arriving at the (back of the) queue, waiting in the queue (essentially the backlog of work), and being served at the front of the queue. They are applied in a wide variety of situations that may be encountered in business, commerce, industry, health care, public service, and engineering.

Queuing strategies support business decisions and ensure that the right resources in the right amount are available to perform services per desired service levels in the right sequence. Service levels are defined as the percentage of services that can be delivered at the time desired by the customer (Chapter 10). Sequence is the order of events, things, work, and so on.

Why Use Them?

In an ideal world, demand for services would be constant and all of the resources (people, technology, materials, facilities, tools, instructions) necessary to perform the service would be available at the time and in the order of need. In achieving the goal of matching supply to demand, organizations would always operate at maximum efficiency, delivering exactly what was needed, with the exact amount of resources—no more, no less. But for most service companies, the amount and priority of work that must be done varies by the minute, hour, day, and week, while the capacity to respond remains fixed or inflexible.

As customers seek sources of supply to meet their demands they may find the marketplace in one of four states.

Excess demand—Customers can't find a service provider to meet their needs at the time of the need.

For service offerings this means lost business. For internal services, it may mean that vital business transactions or services are not completed, at great cost to the organization.

Demand exceeding optimum capacity—Customers must wait (a lean waste) until capacity becomes available. Service providers may experience tremendous environmental pressure to do more than is possible under normal work conditions, causing those resources to rush or disrupt current services activities, with costly consequences.

Balanced demand and supply—Customer service requirements are met with the optimal combination of resources at the time of need.

Excess capacity—Idle resources add undue cost to the service offering and internal delivery processes.

Queuing strategies enable companies to sequence their activities and resources as they attempt to balance demand with supply.

 ## What skills and concepts do I need to know?

Service Level Objectives

The term service level is used in supply chain management to measure the performance of a system as it attempts to meet customer expectations at the time and place required. To remain viable in the marketplace, a service organization must have enough resource capacity to perform services when they are needed, based on desired service levels. Normally, service levels are balanced against the investment in resources required to achieve it. For example, a 99% service level may require operational costs too high to achieve 100% of the time. In this case, the organization may find that a 95% service level is cost effective without causing customer dissatisfaction.

Example: At any time, a retail store may have an average of five customers waiting in a checkout line. Does this mean that the retail store should open up five more checkout lines to improve service levels? To solve this problem, some retail stores have invested in equipment that allows customers to check out themselves—improving customer satisfaction and service levels while reducing costs. Another solution is to employ forecasting software to best estimate when demand will occur, helping the organization plan staff resources for peak and off-peak times.

 Example: SERV-ALL's call center experiences an average of 100 field service requests between 3 and 5 PM. Does this mean SERV-ALL should have 100 service inspectors ready to go at 3 PM? What do these same inspectors do at other times?

Using queuing strategies, a service organization attempts to balance both good risk and bad risk: the good risk of having resources available at the time of need; the bad risk of lost business and excess costs. Both risk factors significantly affect business success.

Types of Queuing Systems

There are two basic types of queuing systems:

Scheduled—Allocates resources based on a plan of what is to occur and at what time it is to occur. Forecasts, appointments, and datebook systems are examples of scheduled-based systems.

FIFO—Allocates resources based on first in first out service tasks. First come first serve (FCFS) and call back or time-based systems are examples of FIFO-based scheduling.

Understanding Queuing Strategy Factors for Service Delivery

Queuing strategies require that the organization understand the following factors: the demand for its services (type, frequency, source); resource capabilities, availabilities, constraints, and capacity; and work cycle time.

Service demand—By conducting a P_cQ (Chapter 5), a service organization can begin to understand what drives the need for a service, what the sources of these drivers are, how often they occur, whether they are predicted, and whether these drivers can be used to determine the best queuing approach.

 Example: SERV-ALL analyzed its demand and found requirements to service equipment in the field as well as in the shop. It further defined shop demand as one that could use a scheduled queue for standard repairs under thirty minutes and a FIFO queue for more complex repair efforts. Field service used a priority scheme based on impact of equipment downtime to the customer to sequence a FIFO queue.

Service demand frequency—By conducting a frequency analysis, a service organization can determine the likely time that service demands will occur as well as estimate time between service demands. This is essential to determine whether service times can be matched to demand frequency.

 Example: SERV-ALL determined that complex repair demands occurred on a daily basis, at any time during the day. Furthermore, they also determined that it took an average of twelve hours to perform these repairs. This created a challenge to SERV-ALL as it set shift requirements. Sales leadership desired a second shift to increase throughput. Shop leadership desired overtime or next work-day completion. Field operations wanted split shifts with emergency crews for repairs after 10 PM.

Resource capability—Service delivery capability requires one to identify the right combination of resources, such as people, information technology, materials, tools, equipment, facilities, and methods required.

 Example: SERV-ALL determined that an electrician, a mechanic, a service bay with an overhead crane, diagnostic equipment, and repair parts must be available for conducting complex repair applications.

Resource availability and constraints—Resources must be available in the right combination at the desired time to perform service. Any of these resources can constrain or diminish the capacity of the organization.

 Example: SERV-ALL's repair center operator can answer only one call at a time; their eight service bays can only hold one piece of equipment at time.

Work cycle time—Estimating the work effort in terms of time is also a key element of determining capacity for service scheduling. Regarding the time to complete work, some processes can be easily monitored and standardized for both resources and time. Often organizations create work standards for typical service types, thus enabling them to plan and schedule resources more effectively.

 Example: SERV-ALL used field inspectors to estimate repair times for field service work. They compared these to actual hours billed by their subcontractors to improve estimating capabilities. SERV-ALL found that customers were more satisfied if they were given a concrete estimate of timing of the work and how long it would take before the repair crew arrived.

Understanding Shift-Work Impact on Performance

Service organizations constrain supply availability through shift design. This helps establish customer expectations for when service can and will be made available.

 Example: SERV-ALL knows that a significant percentage of its commercial customers operate at least twelve hours a day, with their equipment running twenty-four hours. Nevertheless, it still only operated a single-shift shop repair service. After the queuing analysis was performed, calls for a twelve-hour shift became louder and louder. But humans aren't machines; there are certain factors to consider when designing shift work. Here are a few important ones.

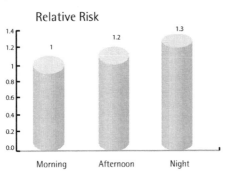

Relative Risks Across Shifts

(Source: Folkard, S. and Tucker, P. Shift Work, Safety and Productivity. 2003) Occupational Machine 53:95-1-1.)

People are circadian—meaning their biological processes recur naturally on a twenty-four-hour cycle—thus, afternoon and night shifts work counter to this natural clock, increasing risk in the workplace.

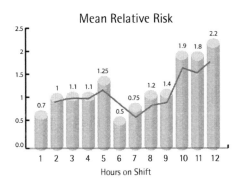

Relative Risks - Length of Shift

Risk varies across the length of the shift. As many work places move to four ten-hour days, it is interesting to note that the risk factors nearly double in hour ten. In sum, the longer we work, the higher the risk factors. Unfortunately, customer service requirements usually don't get easier over a shift.

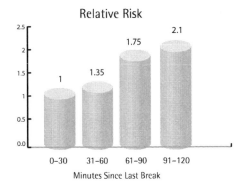

Relative Risk

2.5

2

1.5

1

0.5

0.0

| | 1 | 1.35 | 1.75 | 2.1 |

0-30   31-60   61-90   91-120

Minutes Since Last Break

Relative Risk - Minutes Since Last Break

There is a relative risk between breaks. Once again, sustained efforts without mental or physical breaks increase the risk of improper service delivery. This risk is so real that many governments have enacted meal and break laws that affect shift design.

Many organizations have applied creative "part-time" associate solutions to work shorter hours at potentially challenging times, for instance, hiring students and semiretired people.

Consider the Psychology of Waiting When Designing Queues

Perhaps the most frustrating result of infrequent, inconsistent, and random demand patterns of service offerings is that customers often wait for service. By definition, waiting is a lean waste. However, in practical terms even in the best lean systems someone or something is waiting for a product or service delivery. Here are some well-researched tips for handling customers who must wait in a service queue of any type. (Source: Kampllikar, Dr. Mukta citing work of Edgar Osuna. "Losing 'Waits'" The TMTC Journal of Management)

- ▢ Unoccupied time feels longer than occupied time.

- ▢ Preprocess waits feel much lengthier than in-process waits.

- ▢ Anxiety makes a wait feel longer.

- ▢ Uncertain waits are longer than explained waits.

- ▢ Unfair waits are longer than equitable waits.

- ▢ The more valuable a service, the longer that people are willing to wait.

- ▢ Solo waits feel longer than group waits.

There are two principle strategies for addressing wait times. First is to change the nature of demand through customer expectation management. Second is to improve service capacity through improved capabilities and lean processes.

Example: Managing Customer
Expectations

SERV-ALL knew that the nature of its repair services required strict attention to
detail and ready availability of parts. The normal
work day, 7 AM to 4 PM, provided the lowest risk for
achieving its goal. Knowing that customer demands
varied significantly in both frequency and severity,
they decided to gain some control over the time of
service by providing access to service windows via
the Internet. Customers could reserve inspection
or repair service slots in one hour intervals, twenty-
four hours in advance.

SERV-ALL invested in Computer Telephony Integration (CTI) technology that allows interactions on a
telephone and a computer to be integrated or coor-
dinated. This enabled SERV-ALL to monitor certain
critical assets through remote diagnostic systems
that enabled it to notify customers of impending
"high-risk" situations, prompting the customer to
schedule a service call.

Both of these actions changed the nature of demand,
managed customer expectations, and enabled
SERV-ALL to better estimate resource requirements
for both planned and unplanned events.

Factors for Selecting the Best Queue
for Your Service Application

Most organizations don't think of their activities as
being in a queue or needing to be sequenced. But
queues exist virtually everywhere.

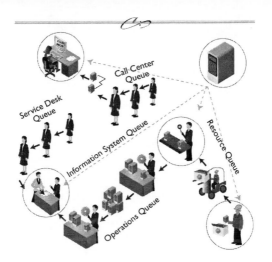

Queues in our Workplace

Examples include call center queues, service desk queues, operations queues, resource (materials, equipment, etc.) queues, and information system queues. Even a to-do list is a queue of things to be done, processing invoices in accounts payable is a queue application, managing the roll-out of new offerings is a queue. Services are typically composed of myriad tasks, accomplished in parallel or serially, and are constrained by the availability of resources. A lean enterprise manages the service queue while attempting to deliver against customer requirements with the optimal use of resources—with no waste. Misalignment of service queue design and associated work or data rules will challenge most lean efforts.

Queue Designs

Consider the following four basic queuing designs when launching your lean service initiative.

FIFO *queue*—First in, first out is designed to support "equal priority" demand, as it occurs, in the order in which the service provider is prepared to respond, but not necessarily when the demand occurs. It requires the service provider to clearly define its services and to have available the typical resources required to perform the service, though not necessarily at the time of demand. Resource availability constrains the queue if demand exceeds capacity. Operating hours, shift design, and work rules will constrain when the service can be delivered. Resource availability and the nature of work will determine the likely time to perform or deliver the service.

Example: SERV-ALL has a FIFO queue for routine repair work performed at their service shops. Customers can wait until the work is completed or SERV-ALL provides courtesy shuttles to and from a customer-designated location. SERV-ALL is mindful of the psychology of waiting and routinely provides the customers with their job's status in the queue.

Scheduled Queue—Scheduled queue attempts to accommodate specific timing of service work in a way that improves the customer's knowledge of when the service will occur, how long it may take, and so on. Scheduled queus require more detailed knowledge of resources and the time required to perform standardized or routine services. This helps the service provider to better define service windows while making resources available at the time of demand.

Example: SERV-ALL provides both a call-in and an Internet-based scheduling system that allows preferred customers to set the drop-off time of their equipment with the expectation that the service work will commence at the time of the drop-off. Based on the nature of work, SERV-ALL provides the customer with the estimated time to complete it. These estimates are based on work standards. SERV-ALL has business rules that it uses to establish preferred customer status and they use this status to manage demand and to drive sales.

Prioritized queue—Prioritized queues give varying levels of importance and, therefore, position in the queue based on the nature of the demand. Typically, priority is based on the service impact on the customer's operations or activity. The impact can be either positive (customer benefits) or negative (customer suffers). Priorities may also be based on compliance or legal requirements; for instance, service work must be completed by a certain date to accommodate warranty requirements, to meet government inspection or reporting requirements, and so on. Both FIFO and scheduled queues may be designed to accommodate customer-stated or internally standardized priorities.

Example: SERV-ALL prioritizes field repair services based on the impact of equipment downtime on customer operations.

Field inspectors work through standardized diagnostics with customers to determine this impact and thus prioritize the work. SERV-ALL has gained increased market share by providing leased or equipment exchange as a swap for downed equipment, minimizing response time and, thus, the customer's downtime. This enables SERV-ALL to return equipment to its service shop for repair based on FIFO.

Combined queues—It is common for service providers to combine various queue designs to maximize the use of resources and give the greatest sense of control to the customer (refer to psychology of waiting discussed earlier in this chapter). Various analysis techniques should be used to answer questions that drive queue designs. For instance:

▫ When does the true demand occur?

▫ Do service demands have varying degrees of response urgency based on impact on the customer?

▫ How well do I understand my service response capabilities: typical resource requirements, typical time to perform services, and so on?

▫ Can service demands be organized to fit an efficient queue design?

▫ What are the standard service practices within my industry?

▫ Can I gain a competitive advantage by providing services closer to demand, based on customer priorities? Which is more efficient and effective than what my competitor offers?

 Example: SERV-ALL combined FIFO and scheduled queues for its service shop and used a prioritized queue for its field service operations. It shifted its work hours to better align its resource availability to likely high-demand periods. It used Quick Change (see Chapter 7, "Visual Management") principles to exchange or lease equipment for field service to mitigate customer downtime, while using a FIFO queue to service the exchanged equipment in a more efficient manner in the shop.

Selecting the Right Queue

So how do you decide which queue is right for you? Here are some factors to consider:

Customer Impact

Does the queue strategy enable you to match supply with demand?

What is the impact of waiting?

Does increased throughput mean increased sales?

Business Impact

Does the queue design require more or less investment in resources than an alternative?

Does the queue selected enable you to achieve continuous flow?

Does the queue selected promote the elimination of lean waste?

Next Steps: Creating Lean Service Supply

Understanding queuing principles and analysis techniques is critical to achieving lean service. This pocket guide is not designed to provide intimate details of queuing strategies and their associated statistical analysis tools. However, in future chapters I will explain and integrate queuing strategies to demonstrate how to achieve lean service delivery.

Chapter SEVEN

VISUAL MANAGEMENT

Visual management is the use of a set of techniques that

- ¤ Expose waste so you can eliminate it and prevent it from recurring in the future.

- ¤ Make your company's service standards known to all employees so they can easily follow them.

- ¤ Improve workplace efficiency through both physical and visual organization.

The essence of visual management is designing and building intelligence into the work environment so that resources can perform efficiently and without error. *Implementing these techniques involves three steps*:

1. Organize both your physical (facilities, equipment, materials, hardcopy files) and virtual (softcopy files, information technology) workplace by using

a method known as the 5 S's (sort, shine, set in order, standardize, and sustain).

2. Ensure that all your required work standards and related information are displayed or easily accessible in both the physical and virtual workplace.

3. Control all your physical workplace and virtual processes by exposing and stopping errors—now and in the future.

What does it do?

Visual management techniques help your company in numerous ways. They serve to

- ☐ Improve the "first-time-through" quality of your services by creating a work environment that:

  - ☐ Prevents most errors and defects before they occur.

  - ☐ Detects the errors and defects that do occur and enables rapid response and correction.

  - ☐ Establishes and maintains standards for zero errors, defects, and waste.

- ☐ Improve workplace safety and employee health by:

  - ☐ Removing hazards.

  - ☐ Improving communication by sharing information openly throughout the company.

  - ☐ Creating compliance with all work standards, reporting deviations, and responding quickly to problems.

- Improve the overall efficiency of your service processes, enabling your organization to meet customer expectations by:

  - Removing clutter and other sources of distraction from both the physical and virtual workplace.

  - Organizing both the physical and virtual workplace so that they support and enhance the flow of activities.

  - Using visual cues, physical constraints, and other techniques to ensure that activities are performed correctly.

- Lowers your total costs through reduction of waste by:

  - Eliminating inefficient workplace activities.

  - Revealing work policies and work practices that unintentionally add time and create inefficiencies.

  - Optimizing the location and management of resources such as materials, instructions, information technology, equipment, and tools.

Why use it?

Creating an organized, efficient, cleaner workplace (physical and virtual) which has clear work processes and standards helps your company lower its costs. Also, job satisfaction improves when your employees' work environment makes it easier for them to get the job done right... the first time.

What areas should I focus on?

You can effectively gain control over your company's service processes by focusing on these areas:

Value-adding activities. Activities that enable the delivery of services to customer expectations.

Information flow. Distribution of the right information, to the right people or technology applications, at the right time and in the most useful form possible.

Resource requirements. Materials, equipment, instructions, information technology, tools, and so on, required to perform services. All work areas and processes should be organized to ensure that the correct resources are available to support workflow and that service tasks are performed as designed.

Source inspections. Inspections to discover the source of errors that cause defects in service processes and to develop visual cues of when they occur (see Chapter 8, "Error Proofing.")

Health, safety, and environment. All work processes, facilities, equipment design, and procedures should contribute to a safe, healthy, and environmentally compliant workplace.

It is most effective to consider these areas of focus as they relate to these six aspects of your service processes:

- ☐ *Incoming Quality*. As a leader, the quality of incoming resources, such as information, materials, equipment, and tools. How do we know that they meet requirements?

- ☐ *Work processes*. As a leader, methods, and instructions that guide the use of resources and performance of services. Are they easily understood and accessible?

- ☐ *Resources*. As a leader, resources such as materials, equipment, information technology, and tools. Are they organized and accessible and do they support the flow of service activities? Can they be obtained easily for use in the service delivery?

- ☐ *Safety and environmental instruction*. Does the service area provide clear instruction for ensuring that the work environment is safe and environmentally compliant?

- ☐ *Information sharing*. Are there physical and/or electronic requirements for sharing information and monitoring its use in service delivery?

- ☐ *The quality of service deliverable*. What standards are we trying to achieve in order to meet customer expectations?

What are the three actuals?
To gain control over your service processes, you must understand the "three actuals":

- The actual place or location at which a service process occurs.

- The actual activities occurring at that location.

- The actual resources being employed (people, instructions, information technology, materials, tools) at that location.

Mapping and diagramming the service process will help you understand all three actuals.

Getting Started

Before you begin to implement visual management techniques, make sure you do the following:

- Elect an employee from each work team to be the "visual management champion." This person will lead the program and remove any barriers his or her team encounters along the way.

- Train all involved employees about the visual management techniques outlined below.

- Tell everyone in the service area that they will be involved in the program. Also give a heads-up to other employees or departments that might be affected by it.

- Create temporary storage ("red-tag") areas for holding resources (materials, files, equipment, tools) that you will remove from service area work sites as you reorganize.

□ Create a location for supplies your team will need as you progress through your visual management program, such as tags, cleaning materials, paint, labels, marking tape, and sign materials.

□ Coordinate with your facilities management and maintenance department and any other departments you might need to call on for help.

□ Make sure that all employees understand and follow your company's safety regulations and procedures as they make changes.

 How to do it?

The 5 S's

To explain the 5 S process, let's begin with the physical workspace.

ONE | Sort

Your goal is to keep what is needed and remove everything else. Sort through the items in your work area, following these steps:

Physical Workspace

Reduce the number of items in your immediate work area to just those you actually need.

Find appropriate locations to position or store all items, keeping in mind their size and weight, how frequently you use them, and how urgently you might need them.

Create a separate storage area for all supplies that you need but do not use every day.

Make a plan for curbing the accumulation of unnecessary items in the future.

Tag all the items you remove from your work area and place the items in a temporary "red-tag storage" area for five days. Use the Sorting Criteria chart on page 141 as a guide for disposing of items or develop your own criteria.

After five days, move any item that you haven't needed to a central red-tag storage area for another thirty days. You, and other departments or work groups in your organization, can then sort through all stored items to decide which are of use and which can be thrown away. Remember to follow your company's retention policy and use a logbook to track what you do with red-tag items.

Tip If employees disagree over how to deal with these materials, try to resolve the conflict through discussion, keeping these criteria in mind: Who uses it? How often is it used? What effect does it have on work performance? Does its location create unintended waste? Establish disposal rules up front for any items that have accounting "book" value, significant acquisition, or replacement costs.

Virtual Workspace

You should also apply the 5 S steps to organizing the virtual work on your computers, the file server, the application server, and so on. In a service environment, it is not uncommon for the physical space to look clean and uncluttered, but your virtual files may be difficult to find in whatever information system you use to manage your work.

The sort process for Information Technology (IT) is similar to that used in a physical sort.

Identify what applications—virtual (softcopies) files, records, multimedia—are relevant for use today or sometime in the future. Compressing and backing up files are examples of processes that can be used to manage infrequently used or older documents.

Use software discovery tools to identify hardware, software applications, and associated files currently loaded on network assets. Other technologies enable discovery of duplicate files, unused files, remnants of old programs, and so on.

Create a red tag area for your virtual files—perhaps a designated space on a server, a backup drive, or a third-party storage service.

With the growth of mobile computing, many workers rely on laptops for both personal and professional use. Be sensitive to both the legal and personal productivity impacts of files stored on these devices when addressing this situation during your sort process.

TWO | Shine

Clean your workplace—eliminate all forms of contamination, including dirt, dust, fluids, and other debris.

Physical Workspace

Eliminate clutter and all other forms of distraction. Often in a service environment, work centers around the processing of information—data processing, face-to-face meetings, phone conversations, e-mails, online collaborative meetings, and so on. Consider your company's information processing activities and how they use work spaces, such as offices, cubicles, and open floor space (at work and at home offices). Also consider the sporadic nature of service work. When you think about how much multitasking service workers must do, it is understandable why a work area can quickly become cluttered.

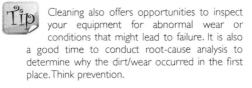

Cleaning also offers opportunities to inspect your equipment for abnormal wear or conditions that might lead to failure. It is also a good time to conduct root-cause analysis to determine why the dirt/wear occurred in the first place. Think prevention.

Once your cleaning process is complete, find ways to eliminate all sources of contamination, clutter, and other distractions and to keep your workplace clean at all times.

Virtual Workspace

Don't forget to defragment your computer system. Rid it of unused registry keys and entries. Delete old files. Yes, cleaning applies to the virtual world as well. And while you are at it, its time to clean your keyboard, your monitor, your mouse, your server fans, filters, and so on.

THREE | Set in order

During this step, you evaluate and improve the efficiency of your current workflow: the steps and motions employees take to perform their work tasks (Chapter 4).

Physical Workspace

Create a map of your workspace that shows where all the office furniture, special equipment, white boards, storage areas, lighting, etc. are currently located. Draw lines to show the steps that employees must take to perform their work tasks (including reaching for items).

Use the map to identify wasted motion or congestion caused by excessive distances traveled, unnecessary movement, and improper placement of tools and materials.

Draw a map of a more efficient workspace, optimally placing every item.

On your map, create location indicators for each item. These are markers that show where and how much material should be kept in a specific place. Once you create your new workspace, you can display location indicators within it.

Quick-Change for Service

When setting resources in order as part of your visual management efforts, consider how you would organize and locate resources so that they minimize wait times between service events. By doing so, you gain the flexibility to meet diverse and ever-changing customer requirements while reducing lead time to perform services. Refer to *The Lean Enterprise Memory Jogger™ for Production* to understand the specific Quick Changeover methodology.

Make a plan for relocating items that need to be moved so you can make your new efficient workspace a reality. (See the "Set In Order Work Sheet" on next page.) As you do this step, ask yourself the following questions:

□ Who will approve the plan?

□ Who will move the items?

□ Are there any rules, policies, or regulations that affect the location of these items?

□ Will employees be able to adhere to these rules?

□ When is the best time to relocate these items?

□ Do we need any special equipment to move the items?

Set in Order Work Sheet

Item to Relocate	Old Location	Proposed Location	Approved By	Assigned To	Relocation Timing	Status
				Date: Dept: Prepared by:		

 As a team, brainstorm ideas for ways to lay out your workspace. If it is impractical or impossible to move an item where you would like to, redesign the rest of the workspace around this item.

Post the diagram of your new workplace layout in your area.

Virtual Workspace

Many companies begin the "Set In Order" process in the virtual world by defining the functional requirements of the work areas or services involved.

Use the enterprise map (Chapter 3) to quickly determine scope of the information flow.

Determine the specific information management requirements of a service or service area, as defined by its value stream map (Chapter 4). The resulting Document Control and Management system design should support these requirements.

Use document control and management systems that enable one to specifically define and ultimately control the placement, retrieval, updating, and purging of work-related files.

Set up your file structures, security levels, access rights, permissions, and so on. These will be of interest to all involved. Review your conflict resolution techniques before you begin this exercise... You will need it if you don't have a clear process for decision making.

FOUR | Standardize

Once your new work environment has been sorted, shined, and set in order, now it is time to document, communicate, and, if necessary, educate your staff on what changes have been made and what "new" practices will be followed.

Physical Workspace

Share information among teams so that there is no confusion or errors regarding:

- ◻ Key locations

- ◻ New workflows

- ◻ New or updated policies, procedures, and standards

 As you begin to use your newly organized workplace, have everyone use Post-it™ Notes to write down their ideas for reducing clutter, eliminating unnecessary items, organizing, making cleaning easier, establishing standard procedures, and making it easier for employees to follow the rules.

Once you have standardized your methods, make your standards known to everyone so that anything out of place or not in compliance with your procedure will be immediately noticed.

Virtual Workspace

Standardizing the virtual workspace may transform your workspace into a Common Operating Environment (COE), in which all members use common file naming conventions, common file locations, and so on.

COE logic is inevitable in larger organizations. The demand for similar or special-purpose software applications and hardware devices invariably grows along with your organization; so must your capacity to support it. To combat uncontrolled and costly growth, many organizations have established hardware and software standards. Discovery tools are often used to ensure compliance to these standards. Don't forget to review these standards, as improvements in technology capability to support a lean environment occur frequently (i.e. a standard software load on a laptop for all employees).

FIVE | Sustain

This is the hardest, and perhaps most important, step of the 5 S process. Old habits die hard.

Psychologists suggest that we rely on old habits mindlessly, setting our brains on autopilot and relaxing into the unconscious comfort of familiar routine. Furthermore, they contend that these old habits, unfortunately, are here to stay. The secret to overcoming this thought barrier is not to focus on old habits, but to consciously guide our thoughts and actions based on new ones. This is the goal of the sustain step: consciously focus on the new way we have organized our workspace.

The gains you make during the first four steps are sustained when:

◻ All employees are properly trained.

◻ All employees use visual management techniques.

◻ All managers are committed to the program's success.

◻ The workplace is well ordered and adheres to the new procedures all your employees have agreed upon.

◻ Your new procedures become a habit for all employees.

Reevaluate your workspace using the Sustain Evaluation Form (see page 140) as needed. Recognize and encourage the achievement of all work groups that are able to sustain their visual management efforts. This will help your company maintain good habits and lead to a cycle of continuous improvement.

Steps to Create New Habits

Identify the habit you would like to change or create. Be very specific. "I want to maintain a neat and orderly workspace" is not specific enough. "I will create a file and a location for every document I desire to retain" is more specific.

Describe the positive benefits of the changed habit, such as, "I will be able to find what I need at a moment's notice!" Keep reminders of these benefits nearby.

Conversely, describe the negative consequences of not adopting the new habit, such as, "Customers will have to wait as I search for information, leading to their dissatisfaction." Keep reminders of these consequences nearby.

Commit to your new habit for a minimum of twenty-one days. Research tells us that it takes a minimum of three weeks to develop a new habit.

Virtual Workspace

The 5 S Blog. Why not? Consider establishing a blog that will enable quick feedback on your new work

organization and include visual management techniques employed. The keeper of the blog needs to be supported by an active team and a feedback structure that reinforces new habits and visual work processes, and that drives continuous improvement.

Sustain Evaluation Form		
Visual Management "Sustain" Evaluation	**Yes/ No**	**Comments**
Sort	• Are all items in the work area necessary? • Have unnecessary items been red-tagged? • Have red-tagged items been removed?	Yes	All moved to red-tag area
Shine	• Have all areas been cleaned? • Has a cleaning schedule been established?	Yes	Schedule set; training under way
Set in Order	• Is the location for every item in the work area defined? • Is every item in its defined location?		
Standardize	• Have standards been established? • Are standards posted? • Have company-wide standards been adopted in the area?		
Sustain	• Is the evaluation being completed on a regular basis? • Are all schedules, such as the cleaning schedule, being followed?		

Sorting Criteria

Frequency of Use	Action
Never (unneeded)	Throw away
Once a year	Place in storage
Less than once a month	Keep in centralized storage
Once a week	Store in general work area
Once a day or more	Carry or keep at workstation

Questions to ask:

- Why is this item needed?
- What is this item used for?
- How often is it needed?
- Is it needed in this location? Anywhere else?
- How many are needed?
- Who uses it?
- How easy is it to replace?
- What might happen if it were not available when it was needed?
- How much space does it occupy?
- Are there any other reasons why this item should be kept here?

Red tags typically contain the following information. You can adapt this list to best suit your company's needs.

Red Tag Information

Item:
Name:
Quantity:
Identification:
(property control number)
Approximate value:
Date item tagged and reason:
Department, shift, operator:
Disposal method:
Red-tag holding area log-in date:
Holding area removal disposal date:
Authorized by:

Chapter EIGHT

ERROR PROOFING

Error proofing is a structured approach to ensuring quality throughout your entire work processes. This approach enables you to improve your service processes to prevent specific errors—and, thus, defects—from occurring.

What does it do?

Error-proofing methods help you to discover the sources of errors through a structured fact-based problem-solving approach. The focus of error proofing is not on identifying and counting defects (i.e. service activities gone wrong). Rather, it is on the elimination of their causes. There is a distinction between an error and a defect:

□ An error is any deviation from a specified service process activity or task characteristic. Errors cause defects in services.

□ A defect is a specific service characteristic, or the whole of the service delivery, that does not conform to specifications or a customer's expectations. Defects are caused by errors.

The goal of error proofing is to create an error-free service environment. It prevents defects by eliminating their root cause, which is the best way to deliver high-quality services.

Why use it?

Services are typically delivered by a combination of resources, such as people, information technology, equipment, instructions, materials, and tools. Any resource can be a source of error. The more resources required, the more likely it is that errors will occur. For your organization to be competitive in the marketplace, you must deliver high-quality services that exceed your customers' expectations. You cannot afford to deliver defective services.

A lean enterprise strives for quality *at the source*. This means that any defects that occur during one service activity should never be passed on or transmitted to the next activity. This ensures that your customers will receive only defect-free services.

In a "fat" system, any defects that are found are simply consciously or unconsciously overlooked while the service process continues. These defects are often tracked and, if their numbers are high enough, root-cause analysis may be done to prevent their recurrence.

In a lean enterprise, the goal is to match supply to demand exactly while minimizing backlog of work that keeps customers waiting for service. When a defect occurs in a lean enterprise, service processes must stop, causing disruptions in supply... thus forcing the organization to take immediate action to resolve the situation. If this notion is scary to you, then ask the question Why? Obviously, service delivery gaps can be costly if defects occur often. Therefore, it is important to prevent defects before they occur.

SERV-ALL Error Proofing Example

Example: SERV-ALL requires input of a unique equipment identification number prior to commencing service. Ownership, repair history, diagnostic instructions, parts, special tools, and safety cautions are all associated with this number. If the number is missing or entered incorrectly it could potentially cause the wrong assignment of resources, service delays, replacement part order errors, and billing errors. The error proofing challenge: get the right equipment number when the service call is initiated.

What areas do I focus on?

Your organization can achieve zero errors by understanding and implementing the four guiding principles of error proofing:

1. Apply general inspection techniques.
2. Achieve 100% inspection.
3. Use error-proofing devices and software rules.
4. Give immediate feedback.

Guiding Principle 1:
Apply General Inspection Techniques

The first, and most important, element of error proofing is inspection. Most organizations use three types of inspections: source inspection, judgment inspection, and informative inspections.

Source Inspection

Source inspection detects errors in a service process before a defect in the service delivery occurs. The goal of source inspections is to prevent the occurrence of defects by preventing the occurrence of errors.

In addition to catching errors, source inspections provide feedback to employees before further processing takes place. Source inspections are often the most challenging element of error proofing to design and implement.

SERV-ALL Source Inspection

SERV-ALL services all major brands of equipment whose manufacturers provide digital catalogs. These catalogs contain model numbers that SERV-ALL uses to match to specific equipment serial numbers (the serial number contains the model number). When the customer initiates a service call, the serial number is requested by the call center. SERV-ALL's management information system verifies this number two ways before it allows the call center to proceed through the process. The first source inspection validates the serial number against the vendor catalogs. The second source inspection is conducted against past service history with the customer or the customer's location. If there is a match, the call center proceeds through the problem discovery process.

Judgment Inspection

Often referred to as final inspection, during these inspections a quality inspector or service provider compares a final service delivery with a standard or a known customer expectation. If the service delivery does not conform to expectation, it is corrected.

The judgment inspection method has two drawbacks. First, it might not prevent all defects from occurring before final inspection or, even worse, before the customer experiences them. Second, it increases the delay between the time an error occurs and the time a resulting defect is discovered. This allows similar defects to occur in the service process and makes root-cause analysis difficult.

 If you rely on judgment inspections, it's important to relay inspection results to all the earlier steps in your service process. This way, information about a defect is communicated to the point in the process at which the problem originated.

SERV-ALL Judgment Inspection

SERV-ALL's call center flags service requests where equipment serial numbers are unknown. (Serial numbers often are worn off through time or equipment use.) The judgment inspection occurs when a service technician first examines the equipment. By this time the equipment has already been delivered to the repair center. If no number exists the technician has to match the equipment to a model number in a catalog or use his or her personal knowledge based on working on similar equipment.

Informative Inspections

Informative inspections provide timely information about a defect so that root-cause analysis can be conducted and the service process can be adjusted before significant numbers of defects are created.

Typically, these inspections are done close enough to the time of the occurrence of the defect so that action can be taken to prevent further defects from occurring.

There are three types of informative inspections:

1. *Statistical process control* (SPC). This is the use of mathematics and statistical measurements

to solve your organization's problems and build quality into your products and services. When used to monitor product characteristics, SPC is an effective technique for diagnosing process-performance problems and gathering information for improving your service process.

However, because SPC relies on sampling a process characteristic, it can detect only those errors that occur in the sample that you analyze. It gives a reliable estimate of the number of total defects that are occurring, but it cannot prevent defects from happening, nor does it identify all the defective service characteristics that exist before they reach your customers.

2. *Successive inspections.* These inspections are performed after one operation in the service process is completed by employees who perform the next operation in the process. Feedback can be provided as soon as any defects are detected or simply tracked and reported later. (It is always better to report defects immediately.)

3. *Self-inspections.* Service personnel perform self-inspections at their own workstations or areas. If one finds a defect in a service activity, he or she corrects it and takes action to ensure that other defects are not passed on to the next operation or to the customer. The root cause of the defect is then determined and corrected.

 Industrial engineering studies have shown that human visual inspection is only about 85 percent effective. Similar inaccuracies occur when humans directly measure physical properties, such as pressure, temperature, time, and distance. Use electronic or mechanical inspection devices to achieve better accuracy.

 Self-inspection is the second most effective type of inspection. It is much more effective and timely than successive inspection. The number of errors detected depends on the diligence of the service personnel and the difficulty of detecting the defect.

 Wherever practical, empower employees to stop the service process when a defect is detected. This creates a sense of urgency that focuses employees' energy on prevention of the defect's recurrence. It also creates the need for effective source inspections and self-inspections.

SERV-ALL Informative Inspection

SERV-ALL's call center representative is given general guidelines regarding the location of serial numbers of major pieces of equipment by brand, either in warranty documents or on the equipment itself. If the serial number is unknown to the caller, the call center directs the customer to perform an inspection of the equipment identification tag or associated documents.

SERV-ALL monitors how many calls involve missing information that cause a bottleneck in the service delivery process. Types of missing information include incorrect serial numbers, inaccurate or incomplete problem descriptions, assignment of the wrong technician, and ordering the wrong materials. SERV-ALL uses SPC charts to monitor the defects and direct problem-solving activities. This would be a type of informative inspection.

Guiding Principle 2: Achieve 100% Inspection

The second element of error proofing is 100% inspection—the most effective type of inspection. During these inspections, a comparison of actual service to standards is done 100% of the time at the potential source of an error. The goal is to achieve 100% real-time inspection of the potential process errors that lead to defects.

It is often physically impossible and too time-consuming to conduct 100% inspection of all of an organization's service process characteristics. To help you achieve zero defects, use low-cost error-proofing devices and software rules (see the next section) to perform 100% inspection of known sources of error. When an error is found, you should halt the process or alert service personnel before a defect is created.

Zero defects is an achievable goal! Many organizations have attained this level through error proofing. One of the largest barriers to achieving it is the belief that it can't be done. By changing this belief among your employees, you can make zero defects a reality in your organization.

SERV-ALL 100% Inspection

SERV-ALL's management information system acts as a 100% inspection system when it validates all equipment serial numbers against vendor catalogs using software rules for data or field validation.

Guiding Principle 3: Use Error Proofing Devices and Data Validation Rules

The third element of error proofing is the use of devices and data validation rules to make 100% inspection a reality: physical devices and data validation rules for specific data or field validation enhance or substitute for the human senses and judgment. They are designed to improve both the cost and reliability of your organization's inspection activities.

Earlier, we stated that services are typically delivered with a combination of resources, such as people, information technology, equipment, instructions, materials, and tools. Furthermore, any resource can be a source of error. Industry technology providers continue to develop remarkable solutions for detecting and preventing errors. Two principle technologies are useful in the service environment:

◻ Physical devices, which exploit mechanical, electrical, pneumatic, or hydraulic technology to sense, signal, or prevent existing or potential error conditions created by service resources. Physical sensing devices can detect object characteristics by using both contact and noncontact methods. Contact sensors include micro-switches and limit switches; noncontact methods include transmitting and reflecting photoelectric switches.

◻ Data validation rules, which use metadata (data about data) for data or field authentication. For example, a data field requires a number versus text; or catches the mistype of "werd" and correct it to "word" or "weird" based on user preference.

By using physical devices or software rules, you can achieve 100% inspection of errors in a cost-effective manner. These physical devices may or may not be combined with software applications.

Common error proofing devices for service include:

◻ Physical constraints (walls, barriers, pathways) of different sizes that physically limit movement during the service process.

◻ Physical cues that inform service personnel of proper use of resources or conduct of an activity.

◻ Alarms or warnings that a service provider activates when he or she detects an error.

◻ Sensors and other location devices that show the presence and/or absence of service providers, their associated resources (materials, equipment, tools), and their proper position.

◻ Counters—devices used to count the number of service tasks performed, resources required or used, and so on.

□ Checklists, which are written or graphical reminders of tasks, materials, events, and so on.

Common data validation rules for information include:

□ Data and field validation rules that sense the presence and quality of data typically found in software applications. Examples include phone number formats, alpha-numeric fields for addresses, length of descriptions, and required entries (no blanks).

□ Data transmission validation rules that sense the presence and/or quality of data, as well as its sequence as it flows between software applications. Examples include *Unable to process due to missing pin* (personal identification number) or *Source is unauthenticated therefore do not process.*

□ Data workflow validation rules that sense the flow of data according to predetermined work processes. An example is a predefined workflow for a purchase request that does not allow a purchase order to be created unless approved in the correct sequence based on levels of authority.

Such physical sensing devices and data validation rules are the most versatile error-proofing tools available for work processes. Once an unacceptable condition is detected, the error proofing device or data validation rule either warns the service provider of the condition or automatically takes control of the service activity, causing it to stop or correct itself. These warning and control steps, known as regulatory functions, are explained more in the next section.

Setting Functions

Setting functions describe specific attributes that sensing devices or data validation rules need to inspect. The four setting functions described below are effective error-detection methods:

1. Contact methods involve inspecting for physical characteristics of an object, such as size, shape, or color, to determine if any abnormalities exist.

   Example: Kitting template used to ensure that all the right parts and tools are available to perform the service work.

2. Fixed-value setting functions inspect for a specific number of items, events, and so on, to determine if any abnormalities exist.

   Example: Barcode reader used to validate the actual number of items or customers being serviced.

3. Motion-step setting functions inspect the sequence of actions to determine if they are performed out of order.

   Example: Mobile device that records procedural steps as they occur and informs the next step once the previous step is complete.

---

4. Information-setting functions check the accuracy, completeness, and flow of information to authenticate and determine if any errors exist.

    Example: Business rules have established that the grants spending authorization levels are by position. Department supervisor can approve purchase requests up to $500; the purchasing information technology verifies that the person is indeed the department supervisor and validates the purchase amount before converting the request to a purchase order.

SERV-ALL IT Example:

SERV-ALL employs a special diagnostic system that uses the serial number to reference standard equipment configurations and settings. All major brands affix a bar-code to their equipment indicating the full equipment serial number, inclusive of the model number. This barcode enables the diagnostic system to quickly capture equipment numbers and bring up reference settings. Service technicians scan this barcode 100% of the time before beginning services. If the barcode is missing, the serial number is manually typed in and a barcode label is printed and placed on the equipment. The scanner immediately validates the equipment number against the serial number on the service order; if there is a mismatch the barcode reader alerts the technician.

Guiding Principle 4: Provide Immediate Feedback

The fourth element of error proofing is immediate feedback. Because time is of the essence in lean operations, giving immediate feedback to employees who can resolve errors before defects occur is vital to success.

The ideal response to an error is to stop the service process and eliminate the source of the error. But this is not always possible, especially in continuous flow operations (Chapter 5). You should determine the most cost-effective scenario for stopping your work process when an error is detected.

It is often better to use an error-proofing device or data validation rule to improve feedback time, rather than to rely on human intervention.

Methods for providing immediate feedback that use error-proofing devices or data validation rules are called regulatory functions. When an error is detected, the error-proofing device or data validation rule either warns the service personnel of the condition or makes adjustments to correct the error.

There are two types of regulatory functions. The first, the warning method, does not stop the service process but provides various forms of feedback for the employee to act upon. Common feedback methods include flashing lights or unusual sounds designed to capture the employee's attention.

Example: The mistyped "werd" is underlined with a wavy red line. The person can continue to type, but he or she knows that the error has occurred and can fix it before it becomes a defect.

Example: Power to the application server is lost and the battery back-up emits a signal indicating its status. The application server continues to operate, even though the principle source of power has been interrupted.

The second type of regulatory function is called the control method. This method is preferred for responding to error conditions, especially when the error has critical consequences to the customer or the service provider. However, it can also be a more frustrating method for the employee if a service process is continually halted because of the error.

Example: The mistyped "werd" changes automatically to "word" per user preferences. The person can continue to type, unaware that a misspelling occurred. But "werd" really was supposed to be "weird." The user may have to turn off this autocorrect feature if this is a commonly identified error.

Example: The lack of a valid equipment serial number stops the service order entry process.

Warning methods are less effective than control methods because they rely on the employee's or other associate's ability to recognize and correct the situation. If the service person does not notice or react to the error quickly enough, then defective services will still be delivered. However, warning methods are preferred over control methods when the automatic stopping of a service process is very expensive.

Tip: Don't let an error-proofing device sit idle! Unfortunately, this happens all too often when people override sensors, disconnect them, fool them, or completely ignore them. If your employees are tempted to work around an error-proofing device, then install an error-proofing device for the error-proofing device.

Example: Headline reads: "Fueling System Has Little Accountability"

In sixteen months, more than 2,500 gallons of gasoline and diesel fuel were pumped from municipal tanks by people using employee identification codes that don't exist. A gate that restricts night access to the pumps at the city's public works headquarters is controlled by a garage-door opener, but the city has no record of the number of openers it has issued or which employees have them. The mayor said the garage-door openers have been around for fifteen years and some employees probably have "spare ones." Employees using the city pumps must first key in three numbers: a specific vehicle number; a five-digit employee number; and the current mileage. But the system will accept any valid vehicle number, and any number for mileage, including zero, along with any five digits for an employee number. The newspaper review found dozens of instances when cars were filled up with nonexistent employee numbers like "00000." And in some cases, the log showed a vehicle's odometer fluctuating by 100,000 miles between fill-ups, or odometers listed at zero even though the car had been filled up before.

What are some common sources of errors?

Common sources of error include humans, measurements, methods (policies, procedures), materials, machines, and environmental conditions (culture, Mother Nature). Any one of these factors alone, or any combination of them, might be enough to cause errors, which can then lead to defects.

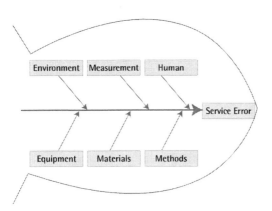

Humans

Unfortunately, human error is an unavoidable reality. The reasons are many, as the following chart indicates.

- □ **Lack of knowledge, skills, or ability.** This can occur when employees have not received proper training to perform a task or if their skill or knowledge level is not verified.

- □ **Mental errors.** These include slips and mistakes. Slips are subconscious actions. They usually occur when an experienced employee forgets to perform a task. Mistakes are conscious actions. They occur when an employee decides to perform a task in a way that results in an error.

- □ **Sensory overload.** A person's ability to perceive, recognize, and respond to stimuli is dramatically affected by the sharpness of the five senses. When an employee's senses are bombarded by too many stimuli at once, sensory overload results, and his or her senses are dulled. This increases the chance for error.

- □ **Mechanical process errors.** Some tasks are physically difficult to do and, thus, are prone to error. They can result in repetitive-strain injuries and physical exhaustion, which are both known to cause errors.

- □ **Distractions.** There are two types of distractions: internal and external. External distractions include high-traffic areas, loud conversations, and ringing phones. Emotional stress and daydreaming are examples of internal distractions. Both types can lead to errors.

- □ **Loss of memory.** Many work tasks require employees to recall information that can be forgotten. In addition, aging, drug or alcohol use, and fatigue can all cause memory loss and lead to errors.

- □ **Loss of emotional control.** Anger, sorrow, jealousy, and fear often work as emotional blinders, hampering employees' ability to work effectively.

Measurements

Measurements must be accurate, repeatable, and reproducible if they are to successfully locate a problem. Unfortunately, measurement devices and methods are as prone to error as the processes that they measure.

Inspection measurement practices, measurement graphs and reports, and measurement definitions are all potential sources of misinterpretation and disagreement. For instance, a measurement scale's being out of calibration can cause errors; a mistyped equation in a spreadsheet analysis can cause errors, data not available in a timely fashion skews reports; and so on.

Don't be surprised if a root-cause analysis points to measurement as the source of an error. An accurate measurement is the product of many factors, including humans, equipment, information systems, and methods.

Methods

Industry experts believe that nearly 85% of the errors that occur in a work process are caused by the tasks and technology involved in the process. The sources of error in a work process are:

◻ *Process steps.* These are the physical or mental steps that people do when performing a service.

◻ *Transportation.* This refers to the movement of

information, people, materials, and technology during a work process.

◻ **Decision making.** This is the process of making a choice among alternatives. Make sure that all your employees' decisions address six basic questions: Who? What? When? Where? How? Why? One company calculated that one billion quality decisions per month were made at its operations. Imagine the opportunity for error!

◻ **Inspections.** These are activities that compare the actual to the expected. As noted above, they are prone to error.

The area of work processes is the one where lean enterprises make the largest gains in error reduction and quality improvement. Concentrate your organizational efforts on this area.

Materials

This factor can contribute to error in these ways:

◻ Use of the wrong type or amount of resource materials, such as parts and tools.

◻ Inherent error in parts and tool designs. A root-cause analysis typically leads back to faulty manufacturing, materials handling, or job specifications practices.

◻ Missing or ill-designed administrative tools

(e.g., forms, documents, and office supplies)
that do not support performance requirements.

Equipment

Equipment errors are classified as either predictable
or unpredictable. Predictable errors are usually addressed by a preventive or scheduled maintenance
plan. Unpredictable errors, which are caused by
unreliable equipment, should be considered when
your organization purchases equipment. If satis-
factory equipment reliability cannot be achieved,
then you must plan other ways to prevent and catch
equipment-related errors.

Environmental Conditions

Poor lighting, excessive heat or cold, and high noise
levels all have a dramatic affect on human attention,
energy levels, and reasoning ability. In addition, un-
seen organizational influences—such as pressure
to perform services on time, every time, internal
competition among employees, and pressure to
achieve higher wage levels—all affect quality and
productivity.

> **Tip** Error proofing devices and data validation
> rules can be used for some, but not all, sources
> of environmentally caused errors. Often, an
> organization's operating and personnel policies must
> be revised to achieve a goal of zero defects.

How do I error proof "red-flag" conditions?

The probability that errors will happen is high in certain types of situations. These so-called red-flag conditions include:

- ◻ *Service variations.* When a high number of variations of a service offering can be delivered by the same person or the same service delivered by a large number of service personnel.

- ◻ *Multiple resource requirements.* When a service process requires multiple types of resources (information technology, parts, special equipment, tools, methods, and so on) at different times, performed by different personnel throughout the delivery process.

- ◻ *Service specifications are rigid and tightly controlled.* Deviation from exact process tasks—precise position or location for a service, latitude, longitude, map-grid, and so on—leads to errors. Resource specifications and critical conditions include work permits, confined space, and personal protective equipment.

- ◻ *Multiple steps.* Most work processes involve many small tasks or sub-steps that must be done, often in a preset, strict order. If an employee forgets a step, does the steps in an incorrect sequence, or mistakenly repeats a step, errors occur and defects result.

□ **Infrequent services.** This refers to a service that is not done on a regular basis. Irregular or infrequent performance of a task leads to the increased likelihood that employees will forget the proper procedures or specifications for the task. The risk of error increases even more when these services are complicated.

□ **Lack of an effective standard.** Standard operating procedures (SOPs) are reliable instructions that describe the correct and most effective way to get a work process done. Without SOPs, employees cannot know the quality of the product or service they produce or know with certainty when an error has occurred. In addition, when there are no SOPs, or if the SOPs are complicated or hard to understand, variations can occur in the way a task is completed, resulting in errors.

□ **Rapid repetition.** This is when the same action or operation is performed quickly, over and over again. Rapidly repeating a task, whether manually or using equipment, increases the opportunity for error.

□ **Poor environmental conditions.** Dim lighting, poor ventilation, inadequate housekeeping, and too many distractions can cause errors.

Always use data as a basis for making adjustments in your service processes. Using subjective opinion or intuition to make adjustments can result in errors—and eventually defects.

Any change in work or resource conditions can lead to errors which, in turn, lead to defects. For instance, degradation of diagnostic equipment produces slow changes that occur without the operator's awareness and can lead to incorrect service delivery.

How do I error proof my service process?

An effective way of error proofing your work processes is to use the 7-Step Problem-Solving Model, a systematic model for solving problems. You use this model to identify errors, create solutions, and prevent the errors from happening again.

During this process, inspections are performed, and error-proofing devices and data validation rules are instituted during Step 4, which involves developing a solution and action plan.

Because all service processes are affected by work design and methods, employees' skill levels and desires, and supporting technology, you must take all of these factors into account during your error proofing activities. *Here is a snapshot of the 7-Step Model:*

The 7-Step Problem-Solving Model

For a complete description, please refer to *The Problem Solving Memory Jogger™.*

7-Step Model

Plan

1. **Describe the problem**

Plan

2. **Describe the current process**

Plan

3. **Identify the root cause(s)**

Plan

4. **Develop a solution and action plan**

Do

5. **Implement the solution**

Check

6. **Review and evaluate the results**

Act

7. **Reflect and act on learnings**

Standard Operations

The term standard operation refers to the most efficient utilization of resources, through the design and execution of work methods and associated protocols.

Resources are composed of the people, processes, materials, facilities, special equipment, tools, information technology, and so on that come together to enable the completion of a work process.

A *method* is a procedure, plan of action, manner in which one conducts business, technique, or systematic arrangement of actions that guide the work process.

Protocols are rules that guide decision making within a method.

What do they do?

When you apply all your knowledge of lean principles to a particular work process to make it as efficient as possible, a standard documented operation is the result. Employees then use this documented process as a guide to consistently apply the tasks they must perform in that work process.

Once you prepare standard operations for your work processes, they serve as the basis for establishing "service level" and "lead-time" expectations for your service delivery.

Standard operations also help your organization's training, performance-monitoring, and continuous-improvement activities.

Why use them?

As discussed in previous chapters of this pocket guide, a big part of making your organization a lean enterprise is to identify different types of waste and find ways to eliminate them. Ultimately, however, it is the correct combination of resources, methods, and protocols that enables your organization to deliver services at the highest possible value and lowest possible operational cost.

Putting together standard operations forces you to break down each of your work processes into definable elements. Each element is analyzed for resource requirements, timing expectations, core actions, and decision-making protocols. This analysis enables you to readily identify waste, solve problems, and provide all employees with guidance about the best way to get things done.

Organizations understand that standard operations are necessary for achieving and maintaining lean work process improvements, resulting in superior service delivery the first time, every time.

How do I develop standard operations for my organization?

The process for developing standard operations involves nine steps. A big part of this process involves gathering information about how your organization's work processes should be done. As such, many of the standard operations steps will take input from the output of other lean techniques such as value stream mapping, service queuing, continuous flow, visual management, and error proofing. There are nine recommended steps for developing standard operations and communicating them to all involved employees:

1. Establish standard operations team(s).

2. Determine your service level objectives.

3. Determine your work sequence.

4. Determine your lead time.

5. Determine process capacity.

6. Determine the standard quantity of resources.

7. Prepare a standard workflow diagram.

8. Prepare a standard operations sheet.

9. Continuously improve your standard operations.

Step 1: Establish Standard Operations Team(s)

Standard operations teams are typically used after an internal service process or an external service offering has gone through a lean analysis. Processes have been newly designed or redesigned based on lean principles and techniques and now must be integrated into workplace or service delivery practices.

If your organization chooses to begin with standardization teams, don't hesitate to use the appropriate lean tool at the right time to create the best flow of activities and use of resources. Remember to coordinate this team effort with your organization's other lean initiatives.

Due to the nature of the steps required to establish and institutionalize standard operations, a team-based approach is best. It is best to have all employees who are affected by a work process involved in the development of standard operations for that process.

Lean organizations understand the need for complete buy-in and support of all work tasks by all the employees involved. This includes not only associates involved with the service delivery process, but, where appropriate, employees who provide enabling capabilities such as human resources, engineering, information technology, and accounting.

Step 2: Establish Your Service Level Objectives

As you begin to standardize your work process, it is important to define the performance requirements the service process must achieve. In the service environment, service level objectives drive process design. Service level measures the performance of a system as it attempts to meet customer expectations at the time and place required. Just like all systems, service processes over time exhibit an average level of performance (mean) as well as its variability (standard deviation). Your goal should be to achieve desired service levels within a given level of variation. *Examples*:

- ◻ All calls answered by third ring, plus or minus one ring.

- ◻ All customers wait on average five minutes, not to exceed fifteen minutes.

- ◻ All orders will be filled 95 percent of the time on the same day, 98 percent by next day. Back-orders to be filled with five working days.

Normally service levels are balanced against the investment in resources required to achieve it. For example, a 99 percent service level may require too high of operational cost to achieve 100 percent of the time. In this case, the organization may find that a 95 percent service level is cost effective without causing customer dissatisfaction.

 Be sure to use the P_cQ analysis (Chapter 5) to help you determine customer demand rates. Calculate takt time as a general guide to process lead-time and capacity design decisions.

To be clear, takt time is owned by the customer (their demand rate) and constrained by the availability of service resources (Chapter 6). The customer demand rate is the average quantity of services expected by the customer over a defined period of time (typically daily). Available service time is the amount of time an organization makes resources accessible to deliver a service. Hours of operations often set the available service time. Takt time is simply the available service time divided by the customer demand rate. Takt time enables your organization to balance the pace of its service outputs to match the rate of customer demand. In the service world, where demand is often sporadic and the lead times for supply are shortened, takt time is the broadest estimate of how often supply of services needs to occur to meet an average demand level over a defined period of time.

The mathematical formula for determining your takt time:

$$\text{takt time} = \frac{\text{available daily service time (i.e., hours of operations)}}{\text{required daily quantity of output (i.e., customer demand)}}$$

Be mindful that different service processes and offerings may have different demand rates, as well as different times of the day (inside and outside of your service window) and, thus, different takt times.

Step 3: Determine Your Work Sequence

A work sequence is the order in which the tasks that make up a work process are performed. A work sequence provides employees with the correct order (consecutive or in parallel) in which to perform their duties. This is especially important for multifunction operators who must perform tasks at various workstations within the standardized or target lead time.

A standard operations combination chart enables your improvement team to study the work sequence and associated lead times for all your organization's work processes. In such a chart, each task is listed sequentially and broken down into manual, automated, wait (batch or process delays), and walk times.

Wait time is not included in a process capacity table because worker idle time has no impact on automated activities or the capacity of a process. However, wait time is included in a standard operations combination chart to identify idle time during which a worker could instead be performing other useful service activities. The goal is to eliminate all worker idle time while not overservicing ahead of schedules or queuing strategies (Chapter 6).

Standard Operations Combination Chart

Standard Operations Combination Chart — Date: August 8th, Page 1 of 1 — Employee: L Camp, Prepared by: L Camp

Type	Process Name	Res	Loc	Avg./D	Cycle	Takt Time	Gap	Manual: --- Auto: ~~~ Wait: <-->
Repair	Service Delivery Process	Test Station	Bay 2	5	244 min.	96 min.	148 min.	

Step	OPERATION DESCRIPTION	TIME (minutes) Manual	Auto	Walk	Wait	Lead Time	Cum. LT	OPERATION LEAD TIME (Takt Time shown; scale 25 50 75 100 125 150 175 200 225 250)
1	Check in Equipment	10		5	1	15	15	
2	Open Service Order	1	1	5	1	7	22	
3	Assign Technician	1	1		1	2	24	
4	Disassemble Equipment	30				30	54	
5	Conduct Diagnostics	1	5		5	6	60	
6	Determine Material Req.	5				5	65	
7	Determine Material Avail.	10	2		2	12	77	
8	Submit Material Request	10	5		5	15	92	
9	Pick up Material			20	15	35	127	
10	Perform Repair	60				60	187	
11	Clean Equipment	15				15	202	
12	Reassemble Equipment	30				30	232	
13	Test Equipment	5	1		1	6	238	
14	Complete Service Order	5	1			6	244	
		183	16	30	31			

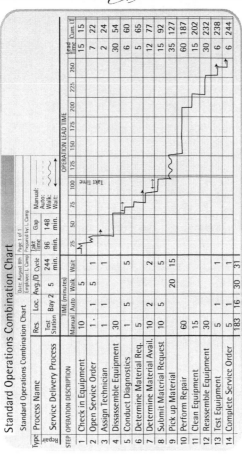

The steps for completing a standard operations combination chart are described below.

1. At the top of a form, like the one shown on the left, indicate the following:

    a. Date on which the work process is being mapped

    b. Number of pages (if the chart is more than one page long)

    c. Name of the employee

    d. Name of the person entering data on the form (if different from the employee)

    e. Service type performed

    f. Name of the process or activity being mapped

    g. Resources required

    h. Location where the service is performed

    i. Amount of services requested (customer demand) per a defined time period

    j. Takt time for the process

    k. Total capacity for the process (see step 3); ideally, this should equal the takt time that you calculated in step 2

2. Gap defined as the difference between the takt time and the cycle time (see step 4) for the work process

3. The block labeled "Time" indicates the type of units the work activity is usually measured in. Activities are normally measured in seconds, but some are measured in minutes or even longer intervals.

4. Number every fifth or tenth line on the graph area to facilitate your recording of activity times. Choose convenient time intervals so that the takt time or the actual cycle time— whichever is greater—is located near the right side of the graph area.

5. Draw a line that represents the activity's takt time. Trace the line with red so it stands out.

6. Sequentially number each operational step in the appropriate column. Steps can include any or all of the following:

    a. Manual operations

    b. Automated operations

    c. Time spent walking from one location to another

    d. Time spent waiting

7. Provide a brief name and description for each step.

8. Note the time required for the completion of each step in the appropriate column.

9. Draw a horizontal line on the graph representing each step, using the following guidelines:

a. The length of the line should equal the duration of the step.

b. The line type should match the action type (see the line key at the top of the sample chart).

c. Each line type should be in a different color, which will make your chart much easier to read.

d. Each line you draw should begin at the point on the vertical time line that corresponds to the actual time the activity begins. It should end at the actual time the activity ends.

10. Indicate lead time for each process step.

11. Indicate cumulative lead time as a cross check to horizontal lines.

Your completed standard operations combination chart should provide you with some useful insights:

❏ If the total time to complete the process or activity equals the red takt time line, congratulations! You already have an efficient work combination in place.

❏ If the total time required to complete the process or activity falls short of the red takt time line, you might be able to add other operations to the activity to use your resources more effectively.

❏ If the total time required to complete the process or activity is longer than the red takt time line, there is waste in your process. To identify where this waste occurs:

¤ Look over the steps in your process to see if any of them can be compressed or eliminated. Perhaps one or more steps can be completed during periods when the equipment operator is waiting for automated operations to be completed.

¤ Look at the movement of employees and materials. Can you reduce or eliminate any of it by relocating supplies or equipment?

Step 4: Determine Your Lead Time

Lead time is the time it takes to successfully complete the tasks required for a work process. It is important to note that a work process's lead time may or may not equal its takt time. Lead time can be broken down into three basic components:

1. **Cycle time.** This is the time it takes to complete the tasks required for a single work process, such as performing equipment maintenance or completing a sales order.

2. **Batch delay.** This is the time a service activity waits while other operations are completed or processed. An example is the length of time the first service request of the day must wait until all the service requests for that day are completed and entered into the system to await approval.

3. **Process delay.** This is how long batches must wait

between the time one operation ends and the next one begins. Continuing the batch delay example, a process delay occurs when a service request backlog in the computer is awaiting approval by a local supervisor, and then by a service management supervisor, and, for high-cost service orders, for upper level management approval. It could take days, if not weeks, to get a service order through process delays.

Lead time analysis can be conducted as part of your value stream mapping activities and/or your completion of the standard operations combination chart.

Step 5: Determine Process Capacity

When comparing lead time to takt time, it may become readily apparent that in order to meet demand requirements, process capacity must be right-sized to match supply to demand (Lean Goal #3). The process capacity table is a helpful tool for gathering information about the sequence of operations that make up a work process and the time required to complete each operation. Ultimately, the process capacity table can help you determine resource capacity.

Steps for creating a process capacity table

1.   Enter service type.

2.   Enter the process name.

3.   Record the net operating time per shift.

4.   Enter the number of shifts.

Date: 8-8-10	Page 1 of 1	Prepared by: L. Camp

Process Capacity Table

Serv. Type	Process Name						
Power System	Service Delivery Process						

		Net Operating Time/Shift (G)	# of Shifts	Max. Out. per shift (H)	Req. Out. per shift	Takt Time	
		480	1	2.0	244 min.	96 min.	

STEP	OPERATION DESCRIPTION	RESOURCES	PROCESSING TIME			Total Cycle (D) (D=A+B+C)	Serv. Capacity per shift (I/J)
			Manual (A)	Walk (B)	Auto (C)		
1	Check in Equipment	Service Rep. SO System	10	5		15	
2	Open Service Order	Service Rep. SO System	1	5	1	7	
3	Assign Technician	Service Rep. SO System	1		1	2	
	Activities Subtotal		12	10	2	24	20
4	Disassemble Equipment	Power Technician, Tools	30			30	
5	Conduct Diagnostics	Power Tech., Diag. Unit	1		5	6	
6	Determine Material Req.	Power Technian	5			5	
7	Determine Material Avail.	Power Tech., Parts System	10		2	12	
8	Submit Material Request	Power Tech., Parts System	10		5	15	
9	Pick up Material	Power Technician	15	20		35	
10	Perform Repair	Power Tech. Spc. Equip, Tools	60			60	
11	Clean Equipment	Power Tech. Spc. Equipment	15			15	
12	Reassemble Equipment	Power Tech. Tools	30			30	
13	Test Equipment	Power Tech. Test Equipment	5		1	6	
14	Complete Service Order	Power Tech. SO System	5		1	6	
	Activities Subtotal		186	20	14	220	2.2
	Activities Total		198	30	16	244	3.0

Example based on a continuous flow operation

5. Calculate the maximum output per shift derived from the capacity table.

6. Enter the sequence number of each processing step being performed.

7. Create subtotal lines for grouped activities.

8. Record the operation description, which is the activity being performed.

9. Enter the classification or description of the resource performing the activity.

10. Record the walk time—the approximate time required between the end of one process and the beginning of the next process.

11. Enter the manual time—the time an employee must take to manually perform service activities when an automated activity is not being performed; the manual time includes any known batch or process delays.

12. Record the automated time—the time required for a machine's automatic cycle to perform an operation, from the point when the start button is activated to the point when the finished part is ready to be unloaded.

13. Calculate the total cycle time by adding the manual time and the automated time.

14. Subtotal cycle times by natural groupings of activities.

15. Enter the service capacity per shift (also known as the total capacity)—the total number of

activities that can be performed during the available hours per shift or per day.

16. Record the takt time for the work process in the takt-time box, using the mathematical formula shown earlier in this chapter.

17. Calculate the total capacity of the process by adding all activity subtotal times and dividing the sum by the net operating time/shift.

> **Tip** Complete a process capacity table before you begin making changes such as moving equipment, changing the sequence of your operations, or moving employees' positions and/or changing their job responsibilities. It is important to first know what your current capacity is and what it will be in the new process configuration that you plan.

Determine Activity Drivers and Resource Capacity Requirements

Before you begin rearranging your workplace, modifying or adding information technologies, updating job descriptions, and changing process instructions to accommodate a continuous-flow method, be sure to create a process capacity table to analyze activity drivers and projected resource capacity requirements.

Activity drivers should be validated against the P_cQ analysis to validate their frequency and timing of occurrence.

Negative press has been given to reduction in headcount objective associated with named improvement techniques such as business process reengineering, six sigma, lean, and so on. To be clear, lean continuous-flow methods attempt to optimize the combination of resources to deliver a service. An activity is something you can do. Capacity is how much you can do. A combination of resources—such as people, technology, and equipment—working under process instructions is required to perform an activity. To arbitrarily remove or reduce any of these resources diminishes the ability to perform an activity, which disrupts services and diminishes customer satisfaction. Arbitrary reductions in any resource required to deliver a service are not part of a lean initiative.

Step 6: Determine the Standard Quantity of Resources

The standard quantity of resources is the minimum amount of equipment, materials, instructions, technology, and so on held at or between your work processes. Without having this quantity of completed work on hand, it is impossible to synchronize your work operations.

When determining the best standard quantity of resources that you should have, consider these points:

▫ Keep the quantity as small as possible.

▫ Ensure that the quantity you choose is suitable to cover the time required for performing the service.

□ Make sure that the quantity you choose enables all employees to easily and safely handle the movement of resources like equipment, tools, materials, and so on between service activities.

Step 7: Prepare a Standard Workflow Diagram

A workflow diagram shows your organization's current facility and equipment layout. It also depicts the movement of employees and resource workers during service processes. Such a diagram helps your lean improvement team plan future improvements to your organization, such as continuous flow (Chapter 5).

The information in your workflow diagram supplements the information in your process capacity table and standard operations combination chart. When used together, the data in these three charts provide a good basis for developing your standard operations sheet (see step 8).

There are ten steps for completing a workflow.

1. At the top of the diagram, indicate:

    a. The beginning and end points of the activity you are mapping.

    b. The date the activity is being mapped. The name of the person completing the diagram should also be included.

    c. The name and/or number of the part or product being produced.

Standard Workflow Diagram			Date: August 8th	
Process Sequence	From:	Receipt of Equip.	Service Type: Power System Repair	
	To:	Comp. of Serv. Order	Process Name: Service Delivery	

Customer

Service Desk

Parts Department

Parts Rep

Power Tech

Wash Station

Hold Area

*Parts

Test Bench

Resources	Location	Avg Serv./Day	Cycle Time	Takt Time	Gap	Current Capacity
Electronic Technician, Diagnostics Equipment, Test Station	Bay 2	5	244 min.	96 min.	148 min.	2 per day

2. Sketch the work location for the work process you are mapping, showing the typical resources (equipment, tools, storage, materials, and so on) used in the service process.

3. Indicate the work sequence by numbering the activities by location in the order they occur.

4. Connect the activity numbers with solid arrows and number them, starting with 1 and continuing to the highest number needed. Use solid arrows to indicate the direction of the workflow.

5. Using a dashed arrow, connect the highest-numbered activity to facility number 1. This arrow indicates a return to the beginning of the service process.

6. Place a diamond symbol (◊) at each facility that requires a quality check.

7. Place a pound sign symbol (#) at each facility where safety precautions or checks are required. Pay particular attention to facilities that include rotating parts, blades, or pinch points.

8. Place an asterisk (*) at each location where it is normal to accumulate standard inventory.

9. Enter the takt time for the operation in the "Takt Time" box. Calculate the takt time using the mathematical formula shown in "Step 2: Establish Your Service Level Objectives" earlier in this chapter.

10. Enter the time required to complete a single cycle of the activity in the "Cycle Time" box. Ideally, this time should equal the takt time.

The workflow diagram provides a visual map of workspace organization, movement of materials and workers, and distances traveled—information not included in either the process capacity table or the standard operations combination chart. You can use this information to improve your workspace organization, resequence your work steps, and re-position your equipment, materials, and workers to shorten your cycle time and the overall travel distance. This will help you to achieve your takt time.

Step 8: Prepare a Standard Operations Sheet

Numerous formats exist for creating standard operations sheets. In general, the layout for your sheet should include the components listed below.

- ◻ The header section should contain:
    - ◻ Date
    - ◻ Prepared By
    - ◻ Page Number
    - ◻ Service Type
    - ◻ Process Name
    - ◻ Net Operating Time/Shift
    - ◻ # of Shifts
    - ◻ Maximum Output

- ◻ Cycle-Time should include:
    - ◻ Required Output
    - ◻ Takt Time

- ◻ The work sequence section should contain:
    - ◻ Step Number
    - ◻ Operation Description
    - ◻ Resource
    - ◻ Manual time
    - ◻ Walk time
    - ◻ Automated time
    - ◻ Key points

□ The workflow diagram section should contain a pictorial representation of the work area. (Refer to the workflow diagram discussion in step 7 for details.)

The layout of a standard operations sheet is straight-forward (see diagram on the next page).

Step 9: Continuously Improve Your Standard Operations

After you complete your standard operations sheet, you should retrain all employees who will be affected by these changes to the work process. Don't be surprised if, during this training, employees discover potential opportunities for even greater improvement.

It is through the continuous improvement of your standard operations that your organization can systematically drive out waste and reduce costs. You should review your organization's standard operations sheet(s) on a periodic basis to ensure all employees are in compliance with the new rules.

Standard Operations Sheet

Date: 8-8-10	Page 1 of 1	Prepared by: L. Camp				

Process Name: Service Delivery Process

	Net Operating Time/Shift (G)	# of Shifts	Max. Out/ per shift (H)	Req. Out/ per shift	Takt Time	
	480	1	2.0	244 min.	96 min.	

STEP	OPERATION DESCRIPTION	RESOURCES	PROCESSING TIME Manual (A)	Walk (B)	Auto (K)	Total Cycle (D)
1	Check in Equipment	Service Rep. SO System	10	5		15
2	Open Service Order	Service Rep. SO System	1	5	1	7
3	Assign Technician	Service Rep. SO System	1		1	2
	Activities Subtotal		12	10	2	24
4	Disassemble Equipment	Power Technician, Tools	30			30
5	Conduct Diagnostics	Power Tech., Diag. Unit	1	5		6
6	Determine Material Req.	Power Technician	5			5
7	Determine Material Avail.	Power Tech., Parts System	10		2	12
8	Submit Material Request	Power Tech., Parts System	10		5	15
9	Pick up Material	Power Technician	15	20		35
10	Perform Repair	Power Tech. Spc. Equip, Tools	60			60
11	Clean Equipment	Power Tech. Spc. Equipment	15			15
12	Reassemble Equipment	Power Tech. Tools	30			30
13	Test Equipment	Power Tech. Test Equipment	5		1	6
14	Complete Service Order	Power Tech. SO System	5		1	6
	Activities Subtotal		186	20	14	220
	Activities Total		198	30	16	244

Workflow Diagram

Parts Department · Parts Rep · Wash Station · Test Bench · Customer · Power Tech · Service Desk · Hold Area · *Parts

Example Based on a Continuous Flow Operation

Chapter TEN

LEAN METRICS

Lean metrics are defined as a system or standard of measurement that gauges progress toward the six lean goals of defining demand, extending demand lead time, matching supply to demand, eliminating waste, reducing supply lead time, and ultimately reducing total costs. Lean metrics are often part of a larger company analytics initiative, where analytics is defined as the extensive use of data (statistical and quantitative), explanatory and predictive models, and fact-based management to drive decisions and actions.

What do they do?

Lean metrics help your company to measure its progress toward its lean goals and objectives. When applied to the customer and to your supply chain, they encourage prioritized and integrated improvement efforts in the extended enterprise (Chapter 3).

Why use them?

Lean metrics serve to focus, prioritize, and unify the organization's improvement efforts in achieving customer satisfaction (quality, cost, and delivery), matching supply to demand, reducing waste, and reducing lead time. When combined in an integrated analytics system, an organization can systematically monitor and drive performance improvement efforts.

Analytics Categories

Lean analytics can be classified into four data management categories described by the Balanced Scorecard. The Balanced Scorecard, introduced by Robert Kaplan and David Norton, is designed as a performance planning and measurement framework. When combined with Lean and Six Sigma initiatives, the Balanced Scorecard methodology helps focus the organization on things that matter to the success of the company.

◻ **Customer**—does the organization deliver products and services to the satisfaction of the customer?

◻ **Internal Processes**—are internal processes lean and effective in matching supply to demand?

◻ **Learning and Development**—are motivated and

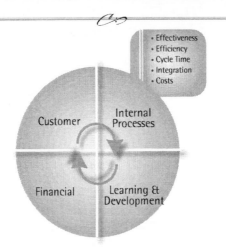

trained employees applying the right skills required to deliver products and services or to perform internal processes as required?

❑ *Financial*—has the company invested wisely in its offerings (marketing, design, development, and delivery) as well as in the resources (people, facilities, equipment, materials, and information technology) of the organization?

This pocket guide will provide examples of customer and internal process metrics. However, the goal question metric (GCM) methodology can be applied to each balanced scorecard category. Furthermore, enterprise mapping (Chapter 3) enables you to map all processes to include financial and learning and development and their associated metrics.

The Goal Question Metric (GQM) Approach

The Goal Question Metric (GQM) approach is an excellent method by which a lean organization can frame and ultimately identify and select its lean metrics. This methodology was designed in a cooperative effort between Victor Basili, Gianluigi Caldeira, and H. Deiter Rombach. The GQM theory, in simplified terms, begins as the organization describes its goals. It asks pertinent questions regarding goal accomplishment and from these questions metrics become apparent.

"Goal" Driven Lean Metrics

To be clear, lean goals are not independent of other business and operational goals. Metrics are designed to measure results that are important to sustaining and growing your customer base through the delivery of service excellence. In balance they are designed to measure process performance so that your organization can deliver these services profitably. Lean metrics must be part of an overarching "analytics" process that not only selects, designs, deploys, and communicates measures, but uses these measures to drive improvement initiatives.

Lean metrics tend to be very specific to the six "integrated" lean goals (Chapter 1). In keeping with the GQM method, these six lean goals should guide metrics development:

1. Define demand for services

2. Extend demand lead time

3. Match supply to demand

4. Eliminate waste

5. Reduce supply lead time

6. Reduce total costs

Classifying Questions That Lead to Lean Metrics

The second step of the GQM method is to ask pertinent questions that provide information about goal accomplishment. The identification and ultimate deployment of the right metric can be a daunting task if this rational approach is not followed. So what questions should be asked? Industry has generically classified the types of questions that we can use to derive lean metrics. These core questions include:

◻ **Effectiveness**—Did we produce the desired or intended result? Did we match supply to demand? Did we achieve customer satisfaction? Were business objectives reached?

◻ **Efficiency**—Did we use resources as designed without wasted time or effort?

◻ **Cycle Time**—Did we execute tasks in the order and time frame as designed?

◻ **Integration**—Did outputs from one activity necessarily become the input to the next activity?

◻ *Total Cost*—How much money was invested, required, or given in payment for something?

SERV-ALL Defines its Metrics at the Enterprise Level

SERV-ALL used the enterprise mapping (see graphic to right) process to define core functions of its operations. It then established goals for each functional area. From these goals it asked the five core questions about effectiveness, efficiency, cycle time, integration, and total cost. The enterprise map shown places the metrics against the functions. It further rated their current performance against the defined metric.

The Basics of Data Collection

Data doesn't contain information until you have at least two pieces of it. Simply put, data is meaningless without comparison. For example, comparison to a goal or a standard, comparison to other data from similar measures over time, and comparison to industry benchmarks.

The Goal Question Metric (GQM) helps us derive information by comparing metrics to goals. Let's say we want to define metrics for achieving the third lean goal of matching supply to demand. We need to dig a bit deeper and ask the fundamentals of the data collection:

Serv-All Core Processes

	Sales	Service Request	Service Delivery - Shops	Service Delivery - Field	Payment Transactions
	Commercial Accounts	Electronic Based Requests	Serv-All Inspections	Serv-All Inspections	Electronic Transactions
	P O I E F M / Trends / E e T I $	P O I E F M / Trends / E e T I $	P O I E F M / Trends / E e T I $	P O I E F M / Trends / E e T I $	P O I E F M / Trends / E e T I $

	Commercial Accounts	Electronic Based Requests	Serv-All Inspections	Serv-All Inspections	Electronic Transactions
Effectiveness	Service Level	Order Accuracy	First Time Quality	Diagnostic Accuracy	Billing Accuracy
Efficiency	Job Standards	Order Entry Timing	Promise Time	Schedule Adherence	Queue Time
Cycle Time	Lead Time	Transaction Time	SO Time	SO Time	Transaction Time
Integration	Order Accuracy	SR Completeness	SO Completeness	Proof of Service	Proof of Payment
Total Costs	Cust. Profitability	Transaction Cost	SO Cost	SO Cost	Transaction Cost

Ratings

Green   Yellow   Red

10 | Lean Metrics 199

□ *What is the purpose of the data we are collecting?* Are we meeting market demands at the time of demand in the quantity demanded?

□ *Will the data tell us what we need to know?* By collecting the wrong data and/or untimely data, we may not be able to determine our effectiveness in matching supply to demand. For example, are we just measuring demand during our normal operating hours of 8:00 AM to 4:30 PM or does demand occur during off-hours?

□ *Will we be able to act on the data we collect?* Even if we gather the right data, did we apply the right analysis techniques to help us interpret it correctly and guide our decisions? For example, if enough demand occurs during off hours, is this sufficient to justify changes in operating hours, changes in staffing to accommodate off-hour support, and so on?

Data Collection Template

It may be helpful to develop a data collection template that ensures that the methods identification, development, and deployment are successful. Consider the use of the following metrics development template to help define and integrate metrics into an overall analytics process.

Lean Metric Template

Metric description	Describe the metric
Lean goal supported:	Determine which lean goals that the metric will be applied to: Define Demand for Services, Extend Demand Lead Time, Match Supply to Demand, Eliminate Waste, Reduce Supply Lead Time, Reduce Total Costs
Analytic category:	Indicate which of the four Balanced Scorecard categories apply: Customer, Internal Process, Financial, and Learning and Development
Question classification:	Indicate which of the five questions you are attempting to answer: Effectiveness, Efficiency, Cycle Time, Integration, or Total Cost
Why was it selected?	Describe the specific purpose of the metric
Who will be using the metric?	Identify who or what will be interpreting and using the metric
When and where will the data be obtained?	Describe the timing and, where appropriate, the location of where data will be collected

How will the data be collected?	Describe the mechanics of the data collection process
What formula (s) will be used for calculation(s)?	Detail the equation(s) to be used
Sample calculation:	Show sample calculations
How often will it be calculated?	Describe the frequency of the metric
How often will the metric be used?	Define how often interpretation of the metric will be conducted and used by the organization

How do I design a data-collection process?

When you design your data-collection process, keep these points in mind:

¤ Make sure that all employees who will collect the data are involved in the design of your data-collection process.

¤ Tell employees that the main driver for data collection is process improvement, not finger-pointing.

- ☐ Use the lean metric template to explain how the data will be used.

- ☐ Design data-collection forms to be user-friendly.

- ☐ When developing a data-collection procedure, describe how much data is to be collected, when the data is to be collected, who will collect the data, and how the data is to be recorded.

- ☐ Automate data collection and charting whenever possible.

- ☐ Involve employees in the interpretation of the data.

Avoid the following pitfalls:

- ☐ *Measuring everything.* Focus instead on the few critical measures that can verify performance levels and guide your improvement efforts.

- ☐ *Misinterpreting data.* Show employees why and how the data was captured. Also tell how the data will be used in your lean enterprise initiative.

- ☐ *Collecting unused data.* Data collection is time consuming. Ensure that all the data you collect will be put to good use.

- ☐ *Communicating performance data inappropriately.* Avoid creating harmful fault-finding, public humiliation, or overzealous competition.

Remember to use the appropriate tools for your analysis. Less experienced teams can use basic tools such as pareto charts, histograms, run charts, scatter diagrams, and control charts. Refer to *The Memory Jogger II*™ for insight on the purpose and use of these tools.

Lean Metrics Examples

Numerous metrics are effectively deployed in a lean initiative. Using the Goal Question Metric (GQM) method will help you identify and select metrics that make sense. The enterprise map can help you place the metrics in the context of the overall functions being performed to deliver services. Here are a few examples of common lean metrics that service organizations find useful.

◻ *Service Level*—measures the ability of a system to meet demand as requested by the customer. As demand-related goals are defined, the service level gives the percentage to which they should be achieved.

SERV-ALL's Lean Metric Template

Metric description	Service level
Lean goal supported:	Define demand for services
Analytic category:	Customer
Question classification:	Effectiveness
Why was it selected?	To determine if customer service demand is being satisfied per customer expectations.

Who will be using the metric?	Call Center, Service Desk
When and where will the data be obtained?	At the time of customer call or interaction with service desk to determine service and/or parts requirements.
How will the data be collected?	Serv-All Business System: Call Center Module backlog monitoring; Service technician input into Service Desk Module
What formula (s) will be used for calculation(s)?	Call center: percent of calls answered by service representative within 3 rings. Avg. number of calls in queue per fixed time intervals.
Service Desk:	Percent of services that can be rendered by customer need time and date. Avg. waiting time before servicing customer order.
Sample calculation:	Percent of Calls w/in 3 rings between the hours of 8:00 AM and 8:59 AM = (15 calls answered w/in 3 rings ÷ 27 calls) x 100 = 55.5 percent
How often will it be calculated?	Instantaneous per individual call or service order
How often will the metric be used?	Summary statistics developed daily, weekly, monthly by service type and location

- **On-Time Delivery**—Percentage of products or services that are delivered per the customer's timing expectation.

SERV-ALL's Lean Metric Template

Metric description	On-time delivery
Lean goal supported:	Match supply to demand
Analytic category:	Customer
Question classification:	Effectiveness
Why was it selected?	To determine if customer product demand is being satisfied per request date
Who will be using the metric?	Parts ordering and service desk
When and where will the data be obtained?	Customer phone calls, Internet-based order, or direct interaction with parts ordering and service desk
How will the data be collected?	SERV-ALL Business System: Parts Ordering Module
What formula(s) will be used for calculation(s)?	Percent of parts (complete line items) delivered to customer per request date. % of orders where promise date does not match delivered date. % of line items delivered early. % of line items delivered late per specified time intervals (+1 day, +1 week, etc.)
Sample calculation:	OTDCust A = (3 lines delivered per request date ÷ 4 total line ordered) x 100 = 75%
How often will it be calculated?	Instantaneous per customer delivery receipt
How often will metric be used?	Summary statistics developed daily, weekly, monthly by order type, part type, and shipping location

☐ **First Time Through Quality**—Percentage of products and /or services that are performed defect-free.

Serv-All's Lean Metric Template

Metric Description	First Time Through Quality (FTTQ)
Lean goal supported:	Eliminate waste
Analytic category:	Customer, Internal Process, Learning & Development
Question classification:	Effectiveness, Efficiency
Why was it selected?	To determine if customer service is performed correctly, the first time, every time.
Who will be using the metric?	Service Desk, Shop Operations
When and where will the data be obtained?	Direct feedback from customer and on-line surveys determining satisfaction with service. Analysis of service per work diagnostic and repair/replace standards.
How will the data be collected?	SERV-ALL Business System: Customer Service Module and Service Order Module
What formula(s) will be used for calculation(s)?	Percent of services delivered per customer quality requirements. % of service orders completed accurately by service desk. % of service orders where initial contact diagnosis matched technician diagnosis. % of service

	orders completed right the first time (right diagnostics, right repairs, right replacements, and so on).
Sample calculation:	Service Order FTTQ week37 = (267 completed SOs – (35 SOs w/incorrect diagnostics + 12 SOs requiring rework due to poor workmanship) ÷ 267 SOs competed) x 100 = 82.4%
How often will it be calculated?	Upon completion of the service order. Per completion of customer satisfaction survey.
How often will the metric be used?	Summary statistics developed daily, weekly, monthly by service type and location.

 It is common to consider time as a customer quality characteristic or to classify first time through quality as a service level metric. You could be correct on both accounts. Don't get hung up on the precise classification of metrics. But do take the definition and application of metrics as a serious exercise that could affect the success of your organization.

▢ **Process Lead Time**—Average time that elapses during the completion of defined service activities. Process lead times consist of task cycle times, batch delays, and process delays.

SERV-ALL's Lean Metric Template

Metric Description	Process Lead Time
Lean goal supported:	Reduce supply lead time
Analytic category:	Internal Process
Question classification:	Efficiency
Why was it selected?	To determine if service processes are performed timely, with no wasted effort or delays, and in the correct sequence to achieve ideal process lead times
Who will be using the metric?	Service Desk, Shop Operations
When and where will the data be obtained?	Through automated time stamping and manual time recording critical milestones in the service delivery process.
How will the data be collected?	SERV-ALL Business System: Customer Service Module, Service Order Module, Mobile Technologies, and Manual Forms
What formula(s) will be used for calculation(s)?	Forecasted times work service estimates provided to customer. Actual times captured or recorded against work activities. Comparison of forecast to actual times.
Sample calculation:	Power Source Replacement Order Fulfillment Lead Time = Service Order Completion Lead Time:
10 – Initial Customer Contact	0.25 hrs
20 – Service Order Creation	0.5 hrs

Batch Delay	2.0 hrs
30 – Service Area Assignment	0.1 hrs
40 – Problem Diagnostics	1.5 hrs
50 – Resource Assignment	0.5 hrs
60 – Perform Repair	2.0 hrs
Batch Delay (awaiting materials)	0.75 hrs
70 – Record Activities	0.25 hrs
Total Lead Time	7.85 hrs

How often will it be calculated?	Per service order completion
How often will the metric be used?	Summary statistics developed daily, weekly, monthly by service type and location.

Be mindful that information flow can bottleneck. Data may be held up or not entered into the system until a group of similar activities are completed—this is referred to as a batch delay. Information can be held up between activities due to the timing of the next activity—this is referred to as a process delay (Chapter 5).

You may consider using average lead times for similar service activities to guide lean improvement activities. Use the appropriate statistical techniques to determine wasteful activities.

☐ *Order Fulfillment Lead Time* (OFLT)—The average time that elapses between the receipt of a sales order through the delivery of the product or service and completion of all associated payment and information transactions.

SERV-ALL's Lean Metric Template

Metric Description	Order Fulfillment Lead Time
Lean goal supported:	Reduce supply lead time
Analytic category:	Internal Process, Financial
Question classification:	Efficiency
Why was it selected?	To determine if order fulfillment processes are performed in a timely manner, with no wasted effort or delays, and in the correct sequence to achieve ideal process lead times
Who will be using the metric?	Service Desk, Shop Operations
When and where will the data be obtained?	Through automated time stamping and manual time recording of critical milestones in the service delivery process.
How will the data be collected?	SERV-ALL Business System: Customer Service Module, Service Order Module, Mobile Technologies, and Manual Forms
What formula(s) will be used for calculation(s)?	Actual times captured or recorded against order fulfillment activities.
Sample calculation:	Power Source Replacement Order

Fulfillment Lead Time = Service Order Completion Lead Time:	
10 – Initial Customer Contact	0.25 hrs
20 – Service Order Creation	0.5 hrs
Batch Delay (awaiting scheduling)	2.0 hrs
30 – Service Area Assignment	0.1 hrs
40 – Problem Diagnostics	1.5 hrs
50 – Resource Assignment	0.5 hrs
60 – Perform Repair	2.0 hrs
Batch Delay (awaiting materials)	0.75 hrs
70 – Record Activities	0.25 hrs
80 – Transact Payment	48.0 hrs
90 – Assess Service Satisfaction	0.25 hrs
Total Lead Time	56.1 hrs

How often will it be calculated?	At completion of service billing (inclusive of satisfaction determination).
How often will the metric be used?	Summary statistics developed daily, weekly, monthly by service type and location.

 To focus your team's efforts, consider breaking down the order fulfillment lead time into discrete metrics within each functional area (e.g., sales, service, accounting), as shown in the SERV-ALL example above. Have each functional area develop value stream maps and then focus its improvement efforts on waste elimination and lead time reduction.

□ **Value Creation to Value Destruction Ratio**—Compares the amount of time in your service process spent on value-creating activities to the amount of time spent on value-destroying activities.

SERV-ALL's Lean Metric Template

Metric Description	Value Creation to Value Destruction Ratio
Lean goal supported:	Eliminate waste, reduce total costs
Analytic category:	Internal Process, Financial
Question classification:	Efficiency
Why was it selected?	To determine if service processes are performed with the minimum of value destroying activities.
Who will be using the metric?	Service Desk, Shop Operations
When and where will the data be obtained?	Classification of activities as value creating and value destroying followed by automated time stamping and manual time recording critical milestones in the service delivery process.
How will the data be collected?	SERV-ALL Business System: Customer Service Module, Service Order Module, Mobile Technologies, and Manual Forms
What formula(s) will be used for calculation(s)?	Actual times captured or recorded against order fulfillment activities. Use activity-based costing techniques; apply resource costs to service activities.

Sample Calculation: Power Source Replacement Order Fulfillment Lead Time = Service Order Completion Lead Time:

10 – Initial Customer Contact	VC	0.25 hrs
20 – Service Order Creation	VC	0.5 hrs
Batch Delay (awaiting scheduling)	VD	2.0 hrs
30 – Service Area Assignment	VC	0.1 hrs
40 – Problem Diagnostics	VC	1.5 hrs
50 – Resource Assignment	VC	0.5 hrs
60 – Perform Repair	VC	2.0 hrs
Batch Delay (awaiting materials)	VD	0.75 hrs
70 – Record Activities	VC	0.25 hrs
80 – Transact Payment	VC	48.0 hrs
90 – Assess Service Satisfaction	VC	0.25 hrs
	Total VA Time	56.1 hrs
	Total NVA Time	2.75 hrs

Ratio of VC / VC+VD = $(56.1 \div (56.1 + 2.75)) \times 100 = 95.3\%$

How often will it be calculated?	At completion of service billing (inclusive of satisfaction determination).
How often will the metric be used?	Summary statistics developed daily, weekly, monthly by service type and location.

> **Tip** Many internal services, by traditional lean definitions, are non-value-adding in that they don't directly support the core value stream of the company (Chapter 1). Make sure you use the value-creating and value-destroying definitions when classifying internal service activities.

◻ **Schedule Adherence**—Measures the percentage of services performed per schedule, in the correct amount, sequence, and mix (service type). Metric parameters are defined as:

   ◻ Amount Performance = amount completed ÷ amount scheduled

   ◻ Sequence Performance = amount completed in the correct sequence ÷ amount completed (or amount scheduled)

   ◻ Mix Performance = amount completed in the correct mix (service type) ÷ amount completed (or amount scheduled)

◻ **Thus Schedule Adherence** = Amount × Sequence × Mix Performance

SERV-ALL's Lean Metric Template	
Metric Description	**Schedule Adherence (SA)**
Lean goal supported:	Reduce supply lead time
Analytic category:	Customer, Internal Process
Question classification:	Cycle Time, Integration

Why was it selected?	To determine if operations perform or deliver services per the schedule.
Who will be using the metric?	Service Desk, Shop Operations
When and where will the data be obtained?	SERV-ALL Business System: Service Order Schedule Tracking
How will the data be collected?	SERV-ALL Business System: Customer Service Module and Service Order Module
What formula(s) will be used for calculation(s)?	Amount: % of services (regardless of type) delivered (actual to expected) per time period. Sequence: % of Service orders completed in the designated sequence (prioritized and sequenced queue). Mix: % of Service Order by type (actual to expected).
Sample calculation:	Amount: 95 Actual SOs/100 Forecasted SOs = 95%;

Sequence: 67 performed in sequence = 67/95 = 70.5%;

Mix: 23/25 EMs, 47/50 GMs, 22*/20 CMs = 90/95 = 94.7% (*no credit given for over-servicing). SA = 0.95 × 0.705 × 0.947 = 0.634 or 63.4%

How often will it be calculated?	Daily and weekly
How often will the metric be used?	Summary statistics developed daily, weekly, monthly by service type and location.

ELEVEN

Chapter

KAIZEN EVENT

The Kaizen Event is a focused improvement effort, in which actual changes are implemented, not just recommended. Kaizen events take place in a compressed time, normally lasting 1 to 5 days.

Kaizen Events are also known as Kaizen Blitz, Rapid Improvement Events, or Kaikaku Events.

The term Kaizen is Japanese in origin. The original kanji characters for this word are:

ķ (kai) meaning change, take apart, or the action to correct

O (zen) meaning good

Masaaki Imai introduced Kaizen as a continual improvement philosophy in his book *Kaizen: The Key to Japan's Competitive Success*. He made extensive use of

Shewhart's Plan Do Check Act (PDCA) cycle to structure improvement activities.

In many industries, the need for rapid rates of change stimulated accelerated team activities which came to be known as the Kaizen Blitz or "Blitzkrieg." In Japanese, the appropriate term for this is Kaikaku. Kaikaku is a rapid change event; Kaizen is a smaller incremental change. Kaikaku is revolutionary; Kaizen is evolutionary. To be sure, many organizations have used Kaizen Events to drive revolutionary Kaikaku results.

What does it do?

The Kaizen Event is a structured team-based effort that focuses organization resources, delivers immediate solutions, and accelerates improvement in all aspects of internal operations. It can easily be extended to the organization's supply chain, where rapid process improvements can affect customer satisfaction and operating costs.

Kaizen Events are useful in accelerating the achievement of the six lean goals. Rapid improvement strategies by goal may include:

1. **Define Demand for Service**—accelerates technology deployment that senses, captures, characterizes, tracks, and promptly reports levels and shifts in demand.

2. **Extend Demand Lead Time**—defines and deploys methodologies that improve the visibility of customer demand requirements at the time of demand. These Kaizen Events often require the involvement of customer resources.

3. ***Match Supply to Demand***—rapidly improves service queuing strategies and work flows to match resources to demand requirements.

4. ***Eliminate Waste***—focuses on a particular waste that is part of a bigger lean improvement strategy.

5. ***Reduce Supply Lead Time***—focuses on the value stream to reduce lead times and eliminate non-value-adding activities.

6. ***Reduce Total Costs***—eliminates known cost wastes, without compromising the ability to deliver services or perform internal operations required to meet customer expectations.

Why use it?
Kaizen Events, by definition, enable firms to benefit from lean initiatives more quickly. In today's world, when most, if not all, employees juggle multiple responsibilities, roles, priorities, and tasks, finding time to "just improve it" appears to be an impossible objective. But what effect do chronic problems, perpetual inefficiencies, and complaining customers and employees have on the success of the organization?

Rules of thumb suggest that a well-defined Kaizen Event can improve an operation in nearly one-tenth the time that a multiweek, multimeeting, team-based improvement project would take. It doesn't take much imagination to estimate the wastes incurred in trying to gather resources for a one-hour meeting that occurs once a week for ten weeks, versus simply doing ten hours of project work. The value of ten hours focused on "get it solved" team activities is intuitively obvious.

What skills and concepts do I need to know?

Kaizen Events are team-based efforts. *The Team Memory Jogger™* is an excellent guide to understanding and managing team dynamics.

Kaizen Events are often facilitated events. The pocket guide, *Facilitation at a Glance!* is an excellent resource for lean facilitators who must establish direction and reach agreement in a very intense time-constrained environment.

Kaizen Events are problem-solving events. *The Six Sigma Memory Jogger II™* outlines a very useful Define, Measure, Analyze, Improve, and Control (DMAIC) problem-solving method that should be used to guide Kaizen improvement activities.

Finally, Kaizen Event team members must understand the lean tools covered in this pocket guide in order to focus efforts on achieving one or more lean goals.

How does the Kaizen Event work?

Kaizen Events have defined phases that must be followed to ensure the highest chance for success. These phases typically include preparation, training, implementation, and evaluation and follow-up.

These phases mesh comfortably with the Six Sigma DMAIC method, the Shewhart PDCA cycle, and leverage lean philosophies and methods. In summary, Kaizen Events integrate easily into any programmatic improvement efforts. Its real usefulness is in its ability to set the stage for rapid improvement while solidifying organization support by getting good results now.

Phase 1—Preparation

During the preparation phase, the organization conducts the following activities:

◻ The scope and target area of the Kaizen Event are defined.

◻ Kaizen outcome objective(s) are identified and clearly described.

◻ Team membership and roles are proposed and finalized.

◻ The Kaizen team receives orientation.

◻ Team objectives are validated and updated as required.

◻ Timing and scheduling requirements are established.

◻ Other organizational resources (not on the team) affected by the Kaizen Event are prepared for upcoming events.

◻ Materials, special tools, and equipment are identified and made ready.

☐ Where necessary, lean method checklists are prepared and used to guide team activities.

Scoping the Kaizen Event

Scoping the Kaizen Event should be done prior to the event to ensure clear expectations as to what can be accomplished, by whom.

☐ **Point Kaizen**—a very narrow "point solution" is typically applied to a defined area or work space—for example, applying visual management techniques to a customer service area (Chapter 7).

☐ **Value Stream Kaizen**—a value stream focus (Chapter 4) looks at the entirety of a work process and often bridges multiple workgroups and areas—for example, applying continuous flow designs and methods (Chapter 5) to high-demand customer service orders.

☐ **Enterprise Kaizen**—at the enterprise level (Chapter 3) improvement trends affect many areas and systems, requiring a broader change management and improvement project. Kaizen Events rarely make sense at this level but have been attempted. A more practical approach is for Kaizen Events to be identified as a direct result of enterprise mapping activities.

It is common for companies to formally define various Kaizen Events by their scopes. This improves communication by making it easy for the organization to understand the general nature of the Kaizen Event without necessitating repeated detailed explanations. For example:

- Visual Management Kaizen
- Error Proofing Kaizen
- Continuous Flow Kaizen
- Lead Time Kaizen
- Waste Kaizen

 Area or value stream (multiple areas)? When scoping a Kaizen Event, initial efforts often select an area (a workplace with a defined set of tasks) to work on first, thus using a quick win to gain employee confidence. As the organization matures in its understanding of and confidence in lean tools, it will find that Kaizen Events focused on streamlining, optimizing, and restructuring value streams will net substantial gains in productivity and service excellence.

Setting the Objective of the Kaizen Event

Kaizens can be selected based on very specific organizational objectives, often referred to as top-down approach. Or Kaizens can be recommended by local improvement resources, often referred to as a bottom-up approach. In either case, objectives should be clear and should be linked to one or more lean goal.

In some cases, a business case may have to be developed to justify the investment in a Kaizen Event.

The business case typically requires that the team develop very specific areas of benefit (in financial terms). Likely outcomes that affect that business case are increased throughput; improved capacity utilization, thus better matching supply to demand; improved productivity through better utilization of resources; and decreased costs associated with the elimination of lean wastes.

Typically, as Kaizen scopes expand—from a single task or area to an entire complex value stream—the organizational involvement expands and, ultimately, approval for conducting Kaizen Events reaches higher levels in the organization.

 Be clear on the Scope of the Kaizen Event. In practice, not all Kaizen Events are well defined and result in measurable success. Not all Kaizen Events successfully improve capabilities. In fact, some hurt performance in order to achieve cost objectives. Beware the unintended consequences of the Kaizen Event. During the scoping process, be clear on what business or operational capabilities will be affected.

Selecting Kaizen Team Members

Selecting team members is a well-described process in many improvement initiatives (refer to *The Team Memory Jogger™*). Experience suggests that Kaizen Events are not for the faint of heart as workplace improvements are made "very real" given the speed at which they are initiated. Be sure that team members

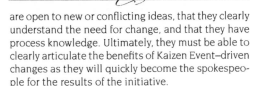

are open to new or conflicting ideas, that they clearly understand the need for change, and that they have process knowledge. Ultimately, they must be able to clearly articulate the benefits of Kaizen Event–driven changes as they will quickly become the spokespeople for the results of the initiative.

A typical mix of resources is required for the Kaizen Event to be successful:

- ◻ People participating in the process

- ◻ People who supply process inputs

- ◻ People who are recipients of process outputs

- ◻ People well-versed in lean methods

- ◻ People who are completely unattached to the process but ask tough questions

Phase 2—Training

During this phase, team members are trained on the applicable lean goals and methods that will be deployed during the Kaizen Event. Don't assume that team members have the same, or correct, understanding of lean principles or methods. To be clear, a lean philosophy lesson is not sufficient, as real changes will by definition be made by the Kaizen Event. Getting it wrong discredits the lean process and may actually cost the organization more than the cost of the effort itself.

Minimum Kaizen Event Training Requirements

When you are training your teams for a Kaizen Event, ensure knowledge of these subjects as minimum insights and capabilities:

◻ Lean goals

◻ Demand analysis

◻ Current state and future state mapping (enterprise, value stream, function-level), as appropriate

◻ Process flow diagramming

◻ Continuous flow

◻ Lean metrics

◻ Team dynamics

◻ Team decision making

> **Tip** Many Kaizen Event proponents suggest that a full day be dedicated to team training. In most cases, this is sufficient if team members have received previous lean and team skills training. Unfortunately, many see this one-day training event as the "only" training event. If this is the case, make sure lean and facilitation experts are available throughout the Kaizen Event to continue the education process as part of Phase 3 and 4 activities.

Phase 3—Implementation

Where to start... mapping the current state or designing the future state? Most organizations begin the Kaizen Event by mapping or diagramming the current state. Certainly, documenting the current state is valuable as a baseline against which to compare before and after results. If Kaikaku—true breakthroughs—is what you seek, consider beginning by clearly defining future state requirements (outputs) and capabilities (things you must be able to do) to meet requirements before you map current state. Often this approach enables your team to reinvent a more streamlined process versus incrementally improving (Kaizen) the existing one.

As future state requirements and capabilities become clearer, try to design these into process flows or process diagrams so all team members can imagine it. You may also want to mock up the work process or area as part of the discovery and design process.

Compare the future state to the current state to determine gaps that must be addressed by the Kaizen team. Identify must-have and nice-to-have changes. Prioritize what can be accomplished in a very short period of time, generally two to three days. Don't throw away the list of other improvement opportunities; they serve as incremental improvements that can be made at a future date, perhaps at another Kaizen Event.

Implement the future state by being mindful of all resources required to deliver new capabilities. What are these resources?

- *People*—define their roles and responsibilities.

- *Methods*—define and document new work content and flows, how decisions will be made, what the new work standards are, etc.

- □ **Data**—define what information is required.

- □ **Information Technology**—define new information system technologies, workflows, rules, etc.

- □ **Facilities, special equipment, tools**—design space utilization, acquire (if necessary) and define special equipment and tool requirements.

- □ **Analytics**—define the measures and the measurement systems that will exist in the new workplace or work process.

Don't allow any one person to dominate the result as this impedes buy-in to new practices. It is possible for an individual to attempt to influence the group's thinking if convinced that his or her proposed solution is the best. Try using the Pugh matrix technique, (*The Design for Six Sigma Memory Jogger*™ page 144) to blend ideas and break through decision roadblocks.

Be aware of groupthink, which discourages creativity and individual responsibility. Groupthink is common among group members who want to minimize conflict and reach consensus without critically designing, testing, analyzing, and evaluating ideas for the future state processes. Unfortunately, staying in one's comfort zone and avoiding embarrassing or heated discussions may result in unsatisfactory results. Establishing ground rules for idea creation and decision making can help you avoid groupthink.

Phase 4—Evaluation and Follow-up

This phase is critical to the success of the Kaizen Event. Be prepared to capture real-time feedback on process changes. Accelerated change process techniques must be deployed to ensure that the new way "sticks." What are some useful techniques?

◻ Create communication channels for employee feedback.

  ◻ Flipcharts in the work area to record feedback

  ◻ Kaizen Event blogs

  ◻ Kaizen Event e-mail address that people can use to share their thoughts

◻ Conduct formal surveys. Surveys should be generated for employee feedback and, if affected, for feedback from customers and/or suppliers. Web-based survey tools make it easy to quickly gather input.

◻ Evaluate existing and new metrics put in place to determine if the Kaizen Event achieved the desired results.

◻ Update the original business case (if it was documented) to justify the Kaizen Event.

◻ Conduct follow-up meetings with team members and affected resources to determine the success of the Kaizen Event and identify any further resource refinements.

Integrating Kaizen Events into an Overall Lean Improvement Strategy

Kaizen Events can easily fall into disfavor if they are not orchestrated as part of a bigger lean improvement strategy. Mapping the enterprise (Chapter 3)—evaluating and rating current capabilities against future business and operational requirements—is a great basis for developing the overarching lean strategy. From this, select target areas or value streams where rapid improvements bring timely results and generate excitement for the improvement process.

Educate your workforce that the Kaizen Event is just one of the team tools your company can use to accelerate improvements. But process improvements on a project-by-project basis are also an important element, especially where bigger system solutions require multiple resources across multiple disciplines.

Finally, a Kaizen Event without connection to lean goals is simply without merit. Kaizen Events aren't change for change's sake exercises. Simply put, they are intended to increase customer satisfaction and improve business and operational performance.

Glossary

Absolute Advantage—a concept of trade, in which an entity offers the exact products and services its customers demand and efficiently produces them, using fewer labor and capital resources than does its competition.

Affinity Diagram—a business tool used to organize ideas and data.

Capability—the ability to do something.

Capacity—the maximum amount that can be perfomed or produced.

Continuous Flow—the sequencing of activities through the service process one task unit of work at a time to minimize delays and reduce the overall lead time.

Demand—the desire of purchasers, consumers, and so on, for a particular commodity or service.

Enterprise Map—a high-level diagram of the internal services activities of an organization.

Goal Question Metric (GQM) Technique—in simplified terms, this begins as the organization describes its goals. It asks pertinent questions regarding the goal accomplishment and from these questions metrics become apparent.

Kaizen Event—structured team-based effort that focuses organization resources, delivers immediate solutions, and accelerates improvement in all aspects of internal operations.

Lean Enterprise—includes all aspects of product design and engineering, going far beyond the factory to the customer.

Lean Production—half the human effort in the factory, half the manufacturing space, half the investment in tools, and half the engineering hours to develop a new product in half the time, as compared to mass production.

Mass Production—the production of large amounts of standardized products including, and especially on, assembly lines.

MTBS (Mean Time between Service) or MTBT (Mean Time between Transactions)—average elapsed time between service (transaction) events typically associated to the same service type for estimating demand characteristics.

MTBI (Mean Time between Incident)—average elapsed time between service events, typically associated to the same customer or resource (equipment, information technology, facility) being serviced.

MTBF (Mean Time between Failures)—average elapsed time between restoration of service following an incident and detection of the next incident. In this case, a big number representing a long time between failures is good because it indicates a reliable service.

OLE (Overall Labor Efficiency)—developed by Kronos, provides insight into workforce productivity, clarifying the impact of both direct and indirect labor so companies can trim costs and recognize opportunities for increasing overall productivity and profitability. Similar to OEE, OLE is composed of availability, performance efficiency, and first-time-through quality as applied to labor resources.

P_cQ Analysis—analysis of ranked services by quantity by customer where P_c stands for Process and Q stands for Quantity.

FCFS (First Come First Serve) Queue—people are serviced by their arrival sequence in the queue.

FIFO (First In First Out) Queue—queues that ensure that the order out of the queue matches the order into the queue; typically following a FCFS strategy.

Functional Requirement(s)—a required capability or output often accompanied by a brief summary and a rationale. This information is used to help explain why the requirement is needed and to track the requirement through the development of the system.

Prioritized Queue—priority schema applied to sequence (order) in queue.

Process—a series of steps or actions that produce a completed order or product.

Process Capacity Table—a tool for gathering information about the sequence of operations that make up a work process and the time required to complete each operation.

Process Delay—the length of time that batches or lots must wait until the next process begins.

Process Route Table—a tool that shows the machines and equipment that are needed for processing a component or completing an assembly process. Aids in grouping manufacturing tasks into work cells.

Production Smoothing—synchronizing the production of your company's different products to match your customer demand.

Productivity—the ratio of output to input. It provides information about the efficiency of your core processes.

Pull System—a production system in which goods are built only when requested by a downstream process. A customer's order pulls a product from the production system. Nothing is produced until it is needed or wanted downstream. Compare to push system.

Push System—a production system in which goods are produced and handed off to a downstream process, where they are stored until needed. This type of system creates excess inventory. Compare to pull system.

Quality Function Deployment (QFD)—a structured process that provides a means to identify and carry customer requirements through each stage of product and service development and implementation. Quality responsibilities are effectively deployed to any needed activity within a company to ensure that appropriate quality is achieved.

Queue—a line or sequence of people, equipment, tasks, and so on, awaiting their turn to be attended to or to proceed.

Queuing Strategies—queuing (sequencing) techniques used to analyze and subsequently match service resources in terms of capability, capacity, and timing to demand requirements of the customer.

Quick Changeover—a method of analyzing your organization's manufacturing processes and then reducing the materials, skilled resources, and time needed for equipment setup, including the exchange of tools and dies. It allows your organization to implement small-batch production or one-piece flow in a cost-effective manner.

Reactive Maintenance—maintenance activities that are performed after a piece of equipment breaks.

Red-Flag Condition—a situation in which the probability that errors will happen is high.

Return on Investment (ROI)—profit from an investment as a percentage of the amount invested.

Root-Cause Analysis—the process of identifying problems in an organization, finding their causes, and creating the best solutions to prevent them from happening again.

Rolled Throughput Yield (RTY)—a metric that measures the probability that a process will be completed without a defect occurring.

Self-Inspection—an inspection performed by the operator at his or her own workstation or area.

Shadow Board—a visual control technique that uses an image of an object to show where it should be stored.

SIPOC (Supplier Input Process Output Customer) Diagram—tool used to identify all relevant elements of a process improvement.

Service—generically defined as work done by one person or group that benefits another.

Service Offering—a service performed for an external customer is an offering.

Service Process—a service performed as part of an internal business process.

Soft-Cost Savings—assets that are freed up so they can be used for another purpose. This contributes no positive change to a company's profit-and-loss statement.

Source Inspection—an inspection that detects errors in the manufacturing process before a defect occurs in the final part or product.

Standard Operating Procedures (SOPs)—reliable instructions that describe the correct and most effective way to get a work process done.

Standard Operations—the most efficient work combination that an organization can put together.

Standard Operations Combination Chart—a tool that enables you to study the work sequence for all your organization's work processes.

Statistical Process Control (SPC)—the use of mathematics and statistical measurements to solve an organization's problems and build quality into its products and services.

Streamline—to reduce the time spent in non-value-added steps, such as downtime, travel time, and inspecting or reworking materials.

Successive Inspection—an inspection that is performed after one operation in the production process is completed, by employees who perform the next operation in the process.

Supermarket System—a stocking system in which materials are stored by the operation that produces them until they are retrieved by the operation that needs them. When a store is full, production stops.

Supply—make services available to someone to satisfy a requirement or demand.

Symmetry—when opposite sides of a part, tool, material, or fixture are, or seem to be, identical. The identical sides of a symmetrical object can be confused during an operation, resulting in errors.

Takt Time—Takt time is simply the available service time divided by the customer demand rate. Takt time enables your organization to balance the pace of its service outputs to match the rate of customer demand. In the service world, where demand is often sporadic and the lead times for supply are shortened, takt time is the broadest of estimate of how often supply of services need to occur to meet an average demand level over a defined period of time.

Total Costs—the sum total of purchase price, acquisition, possession, and disposal costs. Also known as total cost of ownership (TCO) and life cycle costs of a product or service.

Total Productive Maintenance (TPM)—a series of methods ensures that every piece of equipment in a production process is always able to perform its required tasks so that production is never interrupted.

Traditional Cost Accounting (TCA)—an accounting technique that arbitrarily allocates overhead to the products or services an organization creates. It is unable to calculate the actual cost of a product or service.

Value-Added Activities—tasks performed during the production of a product or service, which increase its value to the customer.

Value Creating—all tasks business (enabling), production (core), and ad hoc (devised for the purpose at hand) that enable the organization to successfully deliver services (internal and external).

Value Destroying—any activity or supporting resources that are wasteful and/or are not useful to the performance of necessary core, enabling, and ad hoc processes of the organization.

Value Stream—all the activities that a company must do to design, order, produce, and deliver its products or services to customers.

Value Stream Map—an illustration that uses simple graphics or icons to show the sequence and movement of information, materials, and actions in a company's value stream.

VC/VD (*value creation to value destruction*) *ratio*—a metric that compares the amount of time in your work process spent on value-creating activities to the amount of time spent on non-value-destroying activities.

Variable Costs—costs that vary with production or service/sales levels, such as the costs of raw materials used in the manufacturing process.

Waste—any activity that takes time, resources, or space, but does not add value to a product or service.

Work Combination—a mixture of people, processes, materials, and technology that comes together to enable the completion of a work process.

Workflow—the steps and motions employees take to perform their work tasks.

Workflow Diagram—a graphic that shows your organization's current equipment layout and the movement of materials and workers during work processes.

Work Sequence—the sequential order in which tasks that make up a work process are performed.

Index